BEYOND THE PARK:

An Anthology of Ecological Experiences

AU-DELÀ DU PARC:

une anthologie d'expériences écologiques

T0287164

LABERINTO
PRESS

Beyond the Park: An Anthology of Ecological Experiences
Au-delà du parc: une anthologie d'expériences écologiques

Essays-Essaies

Edited by – Édité par: Ángel Mota Berriozábal

Cover and book design by Cecilia Salcedo

Library and Archives Canada Cataloguing in Publication

Beyond the Park: An Anthology of Ecological Experiences; Au-delà du parc: une anthologie d'expériences écologiques (2024): Essays-Essaies
Edited by – Édité par Ángel Mota Berriozábal

Issued in print and electronic formats.
ISBN 978-1-7770859-5-7

1. Climate Change - The Environment - Canada – Singapore – Mexico – Quebec – Non-Fiction – Fiction.
2. Canadian Literature (English - French).
3. Mota Berriozábal, Ángel – Title.

Printed and bound in Canada

Laberinto Press Ltd
7407 119 Street
Edmonton, AB T6G 1W2
Canada

www.laberintopress.com

BEYOND THE PARK:

An Anthology of Ecological Experiences

AU-DELÀ DU PARC:

une anthologie d'expériences écologiques

Contents

Note from the Publisher

When thinking about our third anthology on the environment and our olfactive memory I never thought it would hit so close to home. I am writing this at the end of July, confined in my house because our province and the country are still burning, and I suffer from asthma. This summer I have seldom left my house, save for ER visits and doctor's appointments. Our country has been on fire from coast to coast to coast for more than two months already. My sense of smell is gone for now. Our anthology editor, Ángel Mota Berriozábal, was ensconced in his house in Montreal for a while like many Montrealers, trying to stay away from the toxic air. Despite, and because of it all, literary creation happens. When I speak of Canada, I speak as an immigrant settler of the diverse territories under Treaty legislation, grappling with the realities of the environmental impact of Colonialism and beyond. The contributors of this anthology are hyphened Canadians who have written their pieces in English or French, Canada's two official languages, complicating the cultural and linguistic idea of the "Two Solitudes." Most of these writers are immigrant settlers, with their own mother tongues. There are more immigrant voices added daily to our conversation on the environment, and yet, there are lots more voices to add to the climate change discourse in the country. Each of the pieces in this anthology, part of a compelling whole, expertly curated by Ángel Mota Berriozábal, honour the name of our press, Laberinto, a place where we meet, and lose each other, in stories and languages.

A note on our cover: we wanted to acknowledge that the current environmental challenges affect not just the present but future generations. With that in mind, we asked our community partners at the Art Gallery of Alberta to invite children aged four to seven years old to submit a piece of art on the subject of "The Park." Dara Armsden-Riddell, Head of Art Education and I selected the winning entry, a sparkling collage of shapes in green and yellow suns and trees by Dominic Godbout, age six and an Edmonton Oilers fan. Our heartfelt thanks to them for trusting us. Dominic's work inspired our designer, Cecilia Salcedo, to give this anthology its bold cover design. The original work is inside the pages of this anthology, carrying the spirit of collaboration, hope for the future, and inclusion throughout our pages.

As always, we hope you engage with our stories through the senses as you consider the possibilities of books and stories to call out the best of our abilities to coexist in harmony. If our previous two anthologies engaged our readers' senses of taste and sight, this one relies on olfactory memories to steer you *Beyond the Park*.

Luciana Erregue-Sacchi
Publisher
Laberinto Press

Foreword to Beyond the Park: An Anthology of Ecological Experiences

Dr. Jenna Butler

Without question, our sense of smell possesses the singular power to sidestep reason and connect us directly to memory, and through memory, to the places and stories we carry with us. For many immigrants, though we may have left our home countries and their distinctive landscapes behind out of necessity or desire, we continue to walk in those spaces in our memories. Writer and naturalist Robert Macfarlane notes in his book *The Old Ways: A Journey on Foot*, "[T]hose places that live on in memory after they have withdrawn in actuality (...)—retreated to most often when we are most remote from them—are among the most important landscapes we possess." This intersection of scent, landscape, and memory is a fertile ground rife with narrative, and it is in this storied earth that *Beyond the Park* begins.

The eleven essays in English and French that comprise this anthology cross continents and time, linked by olfactory experiences that lift the writers from their current homes and transport them back into the landscapes of earlier years, or bring them into closer, more nuanced relationship with the places in which they find themselves in the present. In Kelly Kaur's "The Tree Whisperer," the writer, adrift in Singapore on her first international trip since the start of the Covid-19 pandemic, comes to understand Singapore as a true Garden City through the enthusiastic botanical storytelling of her taxi driver. Rich with the scents of flowers and trees carefully planted by its government over the years, Singapore, a busy country the size of Calgary in which land is rare and precious, is reinterpreted as an urban garden and a park for all its citizens.

Across the world in Mexico, Barbara D. Janusz's "Hammerheads at Balandra Bay" explores an ecological disaster at a pristine beach through the power of scent. The writer and her young son, expecting gorgeous rock formations and long expanses of sculpted sand, encounter instead the half-harvested carcasses left behind by the shark-fishing industry. Thrust into this nightmare landscape, Janusz explores scent and its immediate connection to ecological disaster. The beach, with its decaying pile of hammerhead sharks, is linked inescapably to the fishing industry working just beyond sight, supplying customers around the world who have no firsthand experience of the carnage left behind. For Janusz and her young son, however, the connections are immediate and indelible.

The environmental cost associated with scent is drawn into further sharp relief in Elvira Truglia's essay "The Smell of Joy," in which the writer's multiple chemical sensitivity (MCS), demonstrated through the devastating impact of strong scent on her physical and mental wellbeing, informs how she is able to interact with the urban landscape around her. Truglia explores the social and physical costs of living with a profound sensitivity to chemicals (must she leave the city behind and move to the country, to the mountains, in order to survive?). Where colleagues and family members see only a person sidelined by sensitivity, Truglia wonders whether people like her, "canaries in the coal mine," might instead possess an uncanny ability to identify dangerous environments, places that might be causing us all harm without our even knowing it.

At times, the harms and losses we have endured in our home countries or in the places in which we now live make us question our adaptability and our strength to go on. In Diego Creimer's essay "La baobab de Verdun," two men, immigrants from vastly different places who have sustained catastrophic, violent losses in their lives, bond over the impossibility that is a baobab tree growing on a small island in Verdun, Montreal. Moving between the evocative scents and landscapes of Argentina, Senegal, and Canada, Creimer exposes the emotional freight of the landscapes we carry with us and the ways in which it is sometimes possible to carry the haunted landscapes of both past and present, even when we may feel as though we do not have the strength to go on.

From the beaches of Haida Gwaii to the ice-covered parks of Montreal, *Beyond the Park: An Anthology of Ecological Experiences* takes us through green spaces urban and rural, guided by the fragrances that stir our memories. This evocative bilingual anthology uses scent as a doorway into the landscapes of our lives that are always with us. Through scent, the eleven authors in this anthology speak volumes about the nuanced histories, environmental complexities, and enduring narratives of the places we call home.

Introduction

Au-delà du parc : une anthologie d'expériences écologiques
ou la pensée écologique dans l'espace de la littérature

—

Jean-Pierre Pelletier

L'écologie comme mode de pensée serait-elle une ressource qui se révèlerait au moment de l'éloigner du domaine de la science *stricto sensu* et du constat pour l'engager sur les chemins qui bifurquent et l'ouvrir ainsi à une sensibilité poétique, philosophique et éthique ? On peut alors imaginer une sorte de contrat, une discipline alliant ces trois dernières : une approche philopoéthique de la nature. Le lecteur peut s'interroger sur tous ces rapports et le thème en lisant chacun des auteurs de cette anthologie. Il y a de toute évidence un fil entre chacun de ces récits composant ce recueil : celui du parc et de l'écologie. Laissons aux lecteurs le plaisir de la découverte, l'occasion de plonger dans les différents univers que ce livre leur propose.

Certes, on peut voir un fil qui relie les onze plumes qu'il vous sera donné de lire dans les pages qui suivent. Dans ce livre, cependant, tous n'abordent pas frontalement le sujet qui imprègne de plus en plus l'actualité et les préoccupations de nos contemporains : l'écologie. Y trouve-t-on des inquiétudes, des questionnements liés à l'environnement ?

Existerait-il une méthode d'exploration écologique — écologiste pour certains — qui ne serait ni parole d'augure ou de militant, ni saturation des esprits ? Ce serait le dégel d'une pensée endormie, le regain de vitalité de sensations engourdies, la conversion des consciences à un monde connu auquel on ne faisait plus attention, qu'on ne voyait plus à force d'habitude ou de négligence. Alors pourquoi ne pas imaginer une discipline philopoéthique s'inspirant de l'apport de l'écologie, car qui ne sait plus rêver le monde ne sait pas non plus le changer.

Y a-t-il continuité entre chacune de ces nouvelles, une organicité ?

La littérature en tant qu'art des mots et de la parole peut-elle prendre part à l'imagerie produite et diffusée par les moyens de propagation de l'image aujourd'hui ? Sans doute pas de la même manière et de façon aussi étendue et rapide. Mais elle peut se révéler créatrice d'un imaginaire relevant en propre de la littérature. Et l'on peut se demander comment les préoccupations écologiques interviennent dans le champ de la littérature, comment l'imagerie se transforme en imaginaire.

Voilà, peut-être, ce que les lecteurs découvriront dans ce recueil. À eux d'en juger. Et voilà sans doute ce que chacun des auteurs cherche à réaliser, chacun à sa manière.

Et y a-t-il continuité entre les parcs, pour paraphraser la brévissime nouvelle de Julio Cortázar ?

Ce n'est pas le cas avec les récits que l'on propose ici, sauf dans la nouvelle signée par Ángel Mota Berriozábal, et qui s'intitule « Lorsque Chloé sent les outardes ». Le rêve et le réel semblent parfois se confondre. Et l'idée de l'écologie comme aménagement de la maison («οἶκος», la maison), et de l'espace social comme extension de celle-ci, c'est-à-dire de la Cité, et la nature. L'écologie est aussi une économie. Ici, dans le récit de Mota Berriozábal, les choses ne vont pas tout à fait de soi puisque les relations entre certaines personnes composant la société apparaissent problématiques et floues. Le lecteur verra en lisant que les rapports entre celle qui est désignée sous le nom de la «fille anichinabée» ou l' «Anichinabée» et certains éléments de la société que l'on suppose majoritaire est pour le moins problématique. L' «Indienne» n'est après tout que ce qu'elle est, c'est-à-dire un membre, anonyme, des Peuples premiers, car elle n'est jamais nommée autrement que par son appartenance *ethnique*. Elle n'a pas de nom propre. Les autres, eux, sont nommés, identifiés. On apprend qu'elle est retrouvée morte, on ne sait à cause de qui ni de quoi ; elle reste cependant une *fille*, même pour Chloé, la seule personne des lieux à avoir tenté de l'aborder pour aller à sa rencontre. Par une sorte de métamorphose, qui est ici une expression de la transcendance, Chloé affirme que l'Indienne est devenue une «outarde» (le mot courant pour désigner une bernache au Québec). Un vieil Anichinabé dit même en souriant qu'elle a été «prise» par ces oiseaux, emmenée quelque part dans le sud, où Chloé ira un jour. Le rêve, c'est-à-dire le travail de la fiction, et le réel se confondent une fois de plus comme pour sublimer l'horreur d'une réalité autrement difficile à supporter.

La nouvelles ici évoquées peuvent nous mener vers une sorte de plongée dans la fiction qui pourrait relever de l'allégorie, une emprise de l'imaginaire sur le lecteur et les personnages ; mais on se rend compte que l'immersion dans les univers proposés dans ce recueil ne sont pas absolue, totale : elle implique un esprit qui se trouve dans un état de fractionnement. Ce qui fait penser au monde contemporain, au fragmentaire, à l'éclatement des sociétés dans lesquelles nous vivons.

Cora Siré, l'autrice de « *Siré and I* » (Siré et moi) semble rejoindre le grand Argentin du siècle dernier qui s'amusait à brouiller les pistes entre la fiction, l'écriture de celle-ci et le réel. Le recours à l'imaginaire permettrait de la sorte de remettre en question le monde érigé, gouverné par une raison cartésienne, purement instrumentale, réifiante :

> « Nous aussi, nous perdrons tout au profit du temps et de l'infini. Les portes se fermeront au coucher du soleil, un givre précoce nous enveloppera d'un parfum de larmes **de sorte que tout appartiendra à l'oubli, ou à l'autre**. Prise en otage par le passé et sa quête de vérité, elle m'obligera encore une fois à évoquer Borges : *"***Je ne sais pas lequel d'entre nous écrit ceci**.*"* » (C'est moi qui souligne et traduis).

En effet, l'ombre de Borges veille, traversant le récit de Cora et de son double, qui est peut-être une autre, peut-être la même, sans oublier la figure de la poétesse Alfonsina Storni, pour qui il fallait *écrire pour ne pas mourir*. Nous voilà dans un labyrinthe, suivant la narratrice et son double au fil des déplacements, de la ville Buenos Aires, de pays en pays, d'époques qui se superposent ou se juxtaposent, de l'Europe à l'Amérique et dans ce qui semble le dédale d'un boisé et de la nature. Le récit commence devant des portes pour s'arrêter de marcher un moment se termine aussi devant des portes :

> « Nous perdrons, nous aussi, tout au profit du temps et de l'infini. Les portes se fermeront au coucher du soleil, un froid précoce nous couvrira d'une odeur de larmes afin que tout appartienne à l'oubli, ou à l'autre. Prise en otage par le passé et sa quête de vérité, elle m'obligera une fois de plus à évoquer Borges : « *Je ne sais pas lequel de nous deux écrit ceci.* » (C'est moi qui traduis).

Attardons-nous quelques instants aux titres de certains des textes qui nous sont proposés : « *The Girl Who Fell Into the Sky* » (La fille tombée dans le ciel) de Danielle Guthrie où le récit s'achève par « leurs lumières qui nous survolent dans l'obscurité. » ; « *The Smell of Joy* » (L'odeur de la joie), ou « *The Tree Whisperer* » (Celui qui chuchote aux arbres), « La neige n'a pas d'odeur » et ainsi de suite. Même si le thème du parc n'est pas toujours explicite dans chacun des textes, en revanche la préoccupation pour l'écologie l'est.

Danielle Guthrie, pour sa part, relate l'histoire d'une fille et amie, celle du titre, récit dans lequel ce qui l'assaille d'entrée de jeu ce sont les odeurs de putréfaction rencontrées dans la nature, qu'il s'agisse de l'odeur de la décomposition de matières ou de celle de son amie disparue il y a un peu plus d'une semaine sans que l'on ne sache comment ni pourquoi. La narratrice tente de la retracer. Mais il y a encore une odeur, mais cette fois-ci, c'est celle de la mort... en espérant que ce ne soit pas celle de sa copine... Mais comment savoir au juste... Après neuf jours sans nouvelles de sa part, aucun indice, aucune preuve, comme si elle avait disparu en courant vers un précipice, tombée parmi les étoiles pour y trouver une place, — la sienne. Et voilà la narratrice, seule dans les bois, sous un ciel qui s'assombrit.

Dans le monologue intérieur qu'il nous propose, Hugh Hazelton nous fait remonter la route des souvenirs d'une poétesse d'origine uruguayenne — Maeve, dont il a été l'ami et traducteur — qui s'est trouvée dans la vallée du Saint-Laurent, on ne saura jamais vraiment comment. Mais par des chemins qui bifurquent au gré de ses déplacements sur le vaste continent des Amériques, le lecteur aboutira au parc de l'Île-de-la-Visitation où les cendres de l'autrice finiront par disparaître, emportées par le courant de la Rivière-des-Prairies.

« The Smell of Joy » (L'odeur de la joie), le récit biographique, très factuel, d'Elvira Truglia fait une place au parc du Mont Royal et à divers éléments de la nature, de l'environnement de nos sociétés fortement industrialisées qui sont arrivées, en raison d'une logique productiviste qui a marqué les deux derniers siècles, à engendrer non seulement une civilisation de l'abondance, pour ne pas dire de l'excès, mais à *produire* des maladies caractéristiques de cette même culture et, par ricochet, à affecter gravement la santé des êtres humains qui vivent sur notre planète.

Qu'est devenue la Terre, sinon un parc que les humains ont colonisé ?

Pour Dafne Romero, le parc ne se limite pas uniquement à la terre ferme, mais s'étend au littoral et à la mer : c'est à la fois un jardin et une réserve aquatiques qui recèlent tant de secrets qu'on néglige souvent, qu'on ignore même. Pourtant, le milieu aquatique peut rendre à l'humanité tant de services, ne serait-ce que sur le plan de l'alimentation, qu'on aurait tort de douter de la pertinence ô combien actuelle de l'écologie, c'est-à-dire de cette science, des connaissances précises et des découvertes qu'elle permet. C'est ce que montre et démontre le récit de Romero « A Wild Day ». Il ne s'agit pas simplement d'une journée folle, sauvage, dans la nature, mais aussi et surtout d'une liberté qu'on se donne d'être au plus près de l'état de nature.

Alors que le texte de Romero se situe dans un décor qui est de toute évidence celui de la Côte Ouest du Canada, le récit de Kelly Kaur intitulé « The Tree Whisperer » (Celui qui chuchote aux arbres) nous amène de l'autre côté de l'océan Pacifique, plus exactement dans la Cité-État de Singapour, où un certain Mr. Long, chauffeur de taxi de son état, fait redécouvrir à la narratrice la terre de ses origines, lors d'une balade en taxi dans l'une des artères importantes de la ville.

Les sens, une certaine sensualité, un certain regard sur les choses et la nature, sont très présents dans la description que l'autrice fait de Singapour. En particulier les arbres et les feuilles, celles qui se trouvent à la cime des arbres et ce drôle de phénomène (en apparence) que décrit le chauffeur et qui fait remarquer à la passagère qu'il n'y a pas de vent. L'enthousiasme du vieil automédon emballe à un tel point la narratrice qu'elle se laisse prendre au jeu. Le vieil homme lui demande si elle sent, si elle perçoit le parfum émanant des arbres et des fleurs... Singapour devient alors une sorte de grand jardin. Et c'est sans doute en cela que cette nouvelle rejoint la thématique du départ — l'idée du parc. « *Singapore was a true Garden City* » (Singapour était une véritable Cité-Jardin), dit-elle.

Qu'on se trouve à Singapour ou à Calgary, ville où l'autrice s'est installée, si l'on vit au sein ou près de la nature, c'est ainsi que se révèle son moi véritable, affirme-t-elle.

Dans « La neige n'a pas d'odeur » Marie-Denise Douyon respecte le thème dès le deuxième paragraphe. Cette nouvelle est écrite dans une prose poétique au rythme envoûtant et aux images fortes, scintillant comme la lumière du soleil qui se mire dans la glace, réfléchie par la blancheur de la neige. Ce texte, hommage à la beauté de la nordicité de Montréal et de sa nature « indomptable », est autant un poème par le mouvement qu'il installe qu'un tableau par ses reflets d'argent et d'acier. La ville, à la fois parc humain et lieu de nature, parfois sauvagement violente, est immortelle en dépit des affronts que les éléments lui font subir.

Le récit autobiographique d'Antonio D'Alfonso, « *Ruskin Park* », colle de toute évidence au thème de départ. Il s'agit de réminiscences qui transportent les lecteurs à l'époque de l'enfance, de l'adolescence puis de la prime jeunesse du narrateur dans un Montréal du siècle dernier et dans certains quartiers de la ville : Rosemont, Saint-Michel, etc.

Les parcs sont des lieux de rencontre entre les sexes, des lieux de compétitions sportives entre garçons, des lieux d'une rixe avec le copain d'alors, des lieux d'apprentissages et de socialisation, chemins de traverse et d'initiation aux différents aspects de la vie d'ici pour des fils et des filles d'immigrants. Une sorte d'écologie où des communautés et sociétés humaines vivent dans un environnement auquel elles s'adaptent et qui réagit sur elles.

Barbara D. Janusz est sans doute une écologiste dans l'acception militante, c'est-à-dire une sorte de défenseur humaniste de l'environnement humain et, plus généralement, de la nature en tant que garant d'un bon équilibre pour la société. Elle connaît de toute évidence le lexique approprié pour faire voir, nommer les phénomènes qui émaillent son récit « *Hammerheads at Balandra Bay* » (Les requins-marteaux de la baie de Balandra). Elle sait rythmer une phrase, accumuler les allitérations et les jeux sur les voyelles. Elle sait évidemment écrire, et donc capter l'attention du lecteur. On peut se demander quel lien établir entre son texte et le thème de cette anthologie. On y parle de plage, de l'île de Pâques, de requins-marteaux, comme l'indique le titre, et du destin que l'humanité leur réserve. L'état de décomposition du corps de ces requins pélagiques souvent évoqué par la narratrice conduirait-il le lecteur à poser un parallèle entre l'état putrescent des amoncellements des requins-marteaux et le sort réservé à la nature par l'action de l'humanité ? Malgré le désespoir que la figure de Sisyphe, vieux mythe issu de la Grèce ancienne, peut laisser entendre sous la plume de l'autrice, il est sans doute ici à sa place comme symbole d'un défi à lancer, puis à relever, malgré l'inexorabilité de la descente après la montée. Voyons là un credo pour la sauvegarde et le respect de la Terre et de l'infinie diversité de toutes les formes du vivant qui l'habitent.

Enfin, « Le baobab de Verdun » de Diego Creimer est certainement l'un des récits de ce recueil qui fait preuve d'une grande sensibilité envers la nature et les humains. C'est une histoire touchante, sans mièvrerie, qui fait la part belle au réel et au rêve racontés par l'un de ses personnages, Abdourahmane. Belle et émouvante nouvelle faite de résilience, pour reprendre un mot très en vogue depuis plusieurs années, et qui a l'avantage — je dirais la qualité — de ne pas tomber dans les larmoiements que pourrait susciter le sort de Leopoldo, d'Abdourahmane et de leurs familles. Le parc, ici, ce seraient les berges de Verdun où les deux immigrés se baladent, où ils prennent une chaloupe pour se rendre à la petite île Rock, où Abdourahmane a planté un baobab vingt ans plus tôt. Un baobab au nord du 45e parallèle? L'imagination, une croyance qui défie la rationalité parfois desséchante de certains esprits et une confiance tenace en l'avenir répondent qu'en dépit d'une certaine idée du sens commun, Gaïa peut s'avérer le lieu où se produisent tous les possibles, qu'importe le parallèle, malgré les problèmes et les conflits : elle est le territoire de leur résolution, l'unique, l'irremplaçable Mater Terra.

Cora Siré

Cora is the author of two novels, two poetry collections as well as her latest, a collection of stories, *Fear the Mirror*, published by Véhicule Press in 2021. Her fiction, essays, and poetry have appeared in anthologies and literary magazines in Canada, the US, Mexico, and Europe. Her work has been translated into Spanish and French. She is the cocreator of a short film, *I Want More Life to Love!* inspired by the works and life of the Uruguayan poet, Delmira Agustini. Born in Canada, Cora Siré often writes of elsewheres, drawing on her encounters in faraway places and her family's history of displacement. She lives in Montréal.

Siré and I

When we reach the open gates, we stop walking for a moment. Today's destination is special. She knows that, but I sense she's thinking of that time in Chacarita in the blazing sun when we flitted from the shade of one unfamiliar mausoleum to the next. She created poetry and a dramatic scene out of that experience. Now she's calculating what she will get out of today's excursion.

She can be unpredictable. I've seen her step back, refuse to follow, and insist on another path or destination. I try to be patient as we stand by the entrance, understated compared to the grandiose Doric columns of Chacarita's portico in the brazen metropolis that is Buenos Aires. Today's breeze carries sulphurous emissions of pulp and paper mills downriver from the capital. Harsh smells trouble her even though they may prove useful for her work. She contemplates the road curving uphill, flanked by leafy oaks and maples so tall as to challenge mortality. The stalwart trees are surely cleaning the air I hope we'll soon be breathing.

Perhaps she's daunted by the prospect of the physical effort required to climb the hill. She's a sitter. At her desk, in her red armchair by her stuffed bookshelves, at her kitchen table stirring her many daily espressos, and in the cafés, here in this city and in all the places she has been. I've seen her discuss books and films with great enthusiasm, while I hover in smug silence. I, too, adore coffee, its taste and particularly its aroma, but I don't like sharing her with others. She is animated in such situations, more subdued when she's alone with me. We like the same authors, such as Alejandro Zambra, and filmmakers such as Lucrecia Martel, but she overdoes her passions for such artists, I find, and tends to go on about how great they are in long dramatic sentences that test the patience of her audience. Particularly since her entourage—an eclectic group of poets, philosophers, cooks, carpenters, welders, and watchmakers—may have never heard of the contemporaries she extols. Still, our relationship is not hostile, more frictional in that we might rub each other the wrong way.

Behind us the cars zoom past, followed by a garbage truck grinding its way up the street leaving traces of petrol laced with rotten food. It's possibly the smelly noise she wants to escape when she accompanies me up the road. She will indulge me for now, or at least until the gates are locked at sunset.

We crest the hill and spot, to our left, the crematorium, a squat building perched on a mound with a few black cars in its parking lot. I sniff the air to discern whether there's even a hint of smoke. Scrubbers must have been installed by the chimneys, engineered to prevent charred residues from polluting the surroundings. The prospect of a cremation in progress should not throw us off, here of all places, but it does.

A chipmunk quivers on a rock by the mound, as if in solidarity with our horror, then scampers off. I half expect her to turn as well, hightail it down the road back into the city, triggered by the memory that now comes back to her. We once stood inside that crematorium observing the coffin of a loved one slide on a conveyor belt into the furnace of oblivion. The same loved one who, speaking from experience, used to quote Heine as a warning: *Where books are burned, they will, in the end, burn people, too.*

The quiet interval left by the absence of urban traffic resembles the pausing violins in the piece by Arvo Pärt which caused her to weep during a recent concert. We begin to discern the sparrows, finches, and blackbirds that do not sound like the raucous kweep-kweep of horneros, but as beautiful in their own way. The birdsong prevents her from fleeing, as does the garden beyond the crematorium where rose bushes in hues of crimson, yellow, and green clamber the trellises. Like glorietas, the Spanish more resonant than the harsh, truncated syllabic of arbors.

She's tempted to visit the euphemistical garden of remembrance, I can tell. She likes to linger while I'm always in a hurry, aware that neither of us really belong here, or anywhere else for that matter. My goal is convergence while hers is a quest for truth and meaning. The conflict arises when she wants to drink in a moment, leaving me to worry about what will happen next. I fret that the gates will be locked soon, leaving us, the outsiders, inside. I don't relish being captured here at night by uniformed guards scanning the grounds with high-powered flashlights, or being held hostage by restless ghosts. She, on the other hand, would be drawn to such creepy scenarios as material for her imaginative journeys.

At my instigation, we continue along the road, narrow now, so as to allow only one car at a time, our breathing calmer after the effort uphill. A young woman in a plaid coat is walking her lab who's straining on the leash, the dog's nose discerning all manner of subtleties we cannot detect. Up ahead, on a gravel footpath, an old woman wearing a white headscarf carries a bouquet of black chrysanthemums. I'm glad there aren't too many other interlopers here today, but she looks around as if wondering, *Where is everybody?* She's always in search of an audience.

We pass granite rocks of the Laurentian Shield and glossy marble headstones with intricate carvings of names, dates, and epigraphs. In the distance, an undulating sea of white tombstones stretches across a long lawn all the way to a southern artery. This space has undergone many expansions in its lifetime. The sea of tombstones is one of them, along with, lamentably, a renewed glorification of things military despite recent failed interventions in distant combat zones.

An aerial view taken by a drone would reveal the vast acreage of greenery, trees, and floral flecks, statues, fountains, and ponds, winding pathways and hedges bordering residential properties and avenues. Such a drone would have to surpass even a strong bird, a gull perhaps, soaring toward the Ottawa River. The drone would have to fly very high, in other words, to capture all 160 acres of this property, like an establishing shot in a film. But we remain earthbound, one step at a time, crunching along the gravel with purpose now. She understands our destination is the humble western wall, far from the commemorative sea of fallen soldiers. Still, she does not rebel or abandon me. Perhaps because of the enticing smell-track.

In the best films, there are intervals of silence and of music layered between dialogue and ambient sounds. These intervals establish a mood. As do the odours accompanying the scenes, like the belching furnace inside an industrial refinery, or the cheesy pasta devoured by characters flirting around a table. In a film, such smells must be imagined; here, their palette is as much a part of our reality as our very existence and as diverse as the seasonal vegetation. The spring fragrances of lilac and crabapple flowers that make you swoon, or the cedar and sprucy textures of the coniferous, or the burning freeze of snow much like the powdery surface we once crossed on skis in San Martín de los Andes.

We proceed toward our destination, the low, stone wall in the distance. I'm determined that, this time, we will not get lost like we did in Chacarita searching for Alfonsina Storni's grave. We mistakenly wound up by the bronze statue of Carlos Gardel. How the cliché of the lit cigarette to honour the tango singer provoked her! She blamed me for not being able to find the monument for Storni, a poet whose words and struggles mean more to her than even Borges'.

I stay alive so that she can make her literature. Her words justify my existence. I believe a few of her pages are worthwhile, despite her vices of subversion and aggrandizement, manifested by her propensity to quote other writers, subverting their words as if they belonged to her, such as Storni's claims that she wrote so as not to die.

Her time is elastic, flashing back into haunted memories and forward to futures imagined in her words. She is formulating them now, I can tell, as she envisages extreme weather to come. How tornados will rip through this very spot, knocking over tombstones, decapitating the beech trees, leaving knee-high floodwaters from the rising river and swamps accosting the dead.

I can't quite picture such a scenario. She's the one with the imagination. She has written poems about other graveyards, and novels—spinning off the Heine quote—set in military dictatorships of the late twentieth century when books were, in fact, burned. She has tried to honour the disappeared whether or not they ever were honoured in a place such as this, whether they were dropped from air force planes into the sea, burned, or discarded in mass graves.

While she speculates her fictions, the sun is dropping behind us. Through a grove of magnolias, errant rays flicker like the mirror games she lifted from Borges, along with his self-described theatrical props evoking oblivion. As soon as we stop walking, our bodies cast the one shadow on the grass.

We stand in front of the stone wall. Engraved dynastic plaques are affixed on its surface in an equidistant row, like uniformly hung canvasses in an art gallery. We are interested in the one plaque at the end of the wall. There is no ignoring the words inscribed and the space reserved for future occupants. Our mortality confirmed by the engraving of four letters, Siré.

Our gaze is directed downwards, a slight bow of respect. I'm contained, so she can be the one swaying with grief. For the parents, names inscribed above their years of birth and death. For their arduous journeys, initiated by war and occupation. For their exiles and emigrations, a trajectory that started with displacement from their homes in Estonia, wound through Eastern Europe to Sweden, then ocean-bound across to Uruguay for a short respite before resuming up the Andean spine, beyond the Amazon, Mississippi, and countless other rivers to this sprawling capital named for its own mighty river. She knows that multitudes continue to beat similar paths—people labelled migrants who, in fact, are also refugees—and that every single one of their storied trajectories is unique.

We both remember how, in every language they acquired along the way, the parents always spoke with accents wherever they lived, how they never really belonged anywhere, how they both loved and annoyed each other, their relationship frictional in its own way. History prevented them from being interred in the ground where they were born, and fate intervened to bury them here in Ottawa.

Decades ago, we visited another family grave at a cemetery in Montevideo. It was during the region's last dictatorship, and we were fearful flying in from Buenos Aires. A man on the roof of the airport regarded every passenger taking the steps down from the plane to the tarmac. He spied on us through binoculars to remind us the country was a state of terror, a scene she dramatized in a story. Along with our encounter with the groundskeeper who, even decades after the fact, remembered the death in question and led us to the grave. That episode became the source for all her future obsessions with cemeteries and questions of belonging. I know she will soon dramatize this scene and earlier, the moments when the plaque was cast in red-hot melting alloys that gave off the universal smell of human blood.

When she sits on the grass, I'm forced to sit down as well. There's an honest earthiness here, like mushrooms in a dense forest, from all the corpses decomposing beneath us.

We, too, will lose everything to time and infinity. The gates will close at sundown, an early frost will blanket us in a scent of tears so that *everything will belong to oblivion, or to the other.* Held hostage by the past and her quest for truth, she will again oblige me to conjure Borges: *I don't know which of us is writing this.*

Danielle Guthrie

Danielle writes poetry, short stories, and long fiction in a variety of genres ranging from visceral comedies to dark fantasies. Recently graduated from MacEwan University with her BA in English, Danielle uses her skills to connect with the local writing community in Alberta and build up other writers through her work as an editor for *The Bolo Tie Collective Anthology* and YEGWrites Press. Alongside her anthology work, Danielle is passionate about providing educational editorial feedback for emerging writers by hosting workshops through the Edmonton Public Library and Capital City Press. Beyond writing, Danielle enjoys spending her sunny days outside, drinking coffee, eating croissants, and attempting (but failing) to finish her to-be-read pile. Originally from Vancouver Island, she now resides in Edmonton, Alberta with her dog Coco. She is currently working on her first novel.

The Girl Who Fell Into the Sky

The smell of decay is faint at first, but grows stronger the deeper I travel into the woods, further away from the whirring sounds of semi-trucks and sedans speeding down the highway. A week's worth of worry courses through my body, squeezing my chest and making it hard to breathe. I clutch my sister's phone, dead and useless in my hands, the last connection I have left, pulled out of her F-250 truck with its hood crumpled around the shattered trunk of a jack pine. I instantly recognized the truck as Bri's when I pulled up that night after getting the call. The pink rims and suspension were a dead giveaway. *Truck drivers*, the officer at the scene told me, *they drive too fast and lose control swerving around wildlife.* But Bri wasn't supposed to be on the highway that night. Even if she was, that didn't explain her empty truck cab.

My legs tremble after days of bushwhacking, the mud clinging to the bottom of my boots, sapping my hope and strength through my feet, my calves, my thighs, as if the damp earth itself is telling me to give up, to leave Bri to her mysterious ending. But the thought of never finding her, of never knowing what happened makes my throat swell, my breathing grow ragged. So I press on, my mind rolling around question after question. Why would she leave her truck? Was she drunk? High? Was she concussed and not thinking clearly? Was she scared? Did someone drag her away?

After three days of searching, the Royal Canadian Mounted Police declared her missing, presumed dead. Seven days later, the volunteer-led search parties disbanded, as per regulation. Now, at nine days missing, I keep pressing through the woods, searching groves and swamps, with only the sky above for company.

Scouring the undergrowth of buffaloberry bushes—with their vinegary aroma from fermenting berries—and the wiry branches of swamp birch, I watch the orange glow of the setting sun refract off the remaining alder leaves, making them glisten like shattered mirrors. I didn't have long before I needed to call it a day and head back to the highway turnoff, but here, deep in the woods, the smell is stronger than ever before. The thick, putrid scent reminds me of meat left out too long in the summer sun: sour and tangy. This has to be something, a clue, her way of sending me a message, telling me she's nearby, not to give up.

But what if that smell is her?

I push the thought aside, stooping under a low pine branch as ducks quack in the stormwater pond in the distance. Bri's not dead. She can't be dead. But my mouth grows dry anyways, and no amount of swallowing the oily aroma helps. It has to be animal remains, I tell myself, *maybe a half-eaten rabbit, or a gutted magpie*. But even as I try to convince myself, my heart pounds in my chest like a knocker telling me otherwise: *Thump, thump. Li-ar. Thump, thump. Li-ar.*

Why was she even on this stretch of highway, so far from home? Was she trying to drive off into the sun? Was she heading to the city, a two-hour trip we took to treat ourselves with sugary Starbucks coffees when I first got my licence? I try to remember that night, nine days ago, when Bri asked me to come out with her. To the bar, I think? No, maybe to get groceries, right? But I barely listened, giving her a flimsy excuse, I'm tired, and continuing to lounge on the couch, too engrossed in my phone to look up or say goodbye as she stormed up the steps of the basement suite we rented together after she finished high school. I remember thinking she would thunder up the stairs until she stepped into the sky. Instead, she left through the side door, the lock rattling from her keys.

Guilt swirls through my chest, and I try swallowing it away, but the smell overwhelms me, glazing my tongue and throat like an oily coat, making my stomach roil. I bring my sweatered arm to my nose to block out the worst of it while crossing the clearing, where wheaty heads of foxtail grass whip at my jeans, its seeds snagging onto the denim. Ahead of me, patches of grass are crushed, scattered with half-dried droppings of white-tailed deer and plains bison. Instinctively, I raise my shoulders, an attempt to cover my exposed neck, to protect me from the predators that follow these herds: coyotes and wolves. I hope the smell of decay masks my scent, Bri's scent.

In the centre of the clearing, a paper birch grows with a Dutchman's pipe vining around its trunk, covering it like a green blanket. In some spots, towering above me, the torn dark purple flowers hang limp, but their signature rancid scent permeates the air—the smell of death.

It's not her.

I close my eyes and sigh, out of relief or disappointment, I'm not sure. After nine days with no news, no clues, no evidence, it's as if Bri simply vanished, run off the edge of the plains and fallen into her place among the stars. The stress and anxiety that clenched my body in a tight fist this past week loosen, causing me to unravel all at once.

My shoulders shudder and my chest heaves before I fall to my knees, dropping Bri's phone, and gasping between tears. If only I went with her when she invited me, or if I told her goodbye, or if I rushed out and hugged her before she left, she might still be here, rolling her eyes at a lame joke or singing off-key into our broken karaoke machine. But I didn't, and here I am in the woods, the sky darkening above me, damp and tired and alone.

The orange rays dim to a dusty violet, and the breeze grows colder. I cry in the grass until my body is dry, a husk. It is only by chance that I see the small den to my left, invisible in the grass if I hadn't crushed it under my knees. I lean forward, peering inside the den, expecting to see crowding coyote babies and their mother.

Now, the smell radiates from the den. At the entrance, a torn and dirty pink pompom hangs in a tangle of dead twigs and rocks. A mess of dark hair rests on one end of the den, like a small nest. Further in, lays a shirt—one more plastic than cotton—with a hole in its centre, distorting the peeling graphic, red dye staining its shredded edges. Next to a brown mound, I see a glint of a hoop earring, like the ones I gave Bri for Christmas last year that she wore every day since.

It can't be Bri. I shake my head, trying to clear the image before me. It has to be someone else, something else. But the longer I stare, the more evidence appears before me: her pink lanyard, her pair of favourite frayed jeans, her pink lacquered nails.

My mouth falls open as I breathe in sharply and the scent races inside me, smothering every pore of my body until it contaminates me, until I am also decaying from the inside out. Bile burns the back of my throat while saliva pools over my tongue, but everything tastes sour, like rot.

I scramble away, the knees of my jeans damp, my hands prickling from the scattered rocks and pine needles, and the den falls from sight, as if the ground itself is a mouth, devouring Bri whole.

A shiver courses through my body. Numbly, I get to my feet and run, without looking back, racing out of the clearing as the trees and bushes scratch my face, their twigs clutching my clothes, trying to keep me in the woods. The wind whistles through the leaves, whispering in my ear to join it in the sky, to join my sister, but I push on, stumbling in the rising darkness. My mind spins, replaying one word like a skipping record: *Bri, Bri, Bri.*

I burst from the woods and stumble into the ditch lining the highway, the dry grass prickling my skin, and I retch out the rancidity from inside my body, burning my stomach and throat.

In the grass, mixed in with my vomit, a small piece of red plastic reflects the beam of passing drivers. A fragment of a taillight.

I look behind me, where I came out from the woods, and see a pine stump, its jagged top like a broken toothpick stuck up in the earth, and in front of it, two long scars from tire marks.

The little strength I had leaves me as I slump to the ground. The few stars in the sky swirl above me, and the pounding in my head turns my brain into an anvil, pain coursing through my body with every hit.

From the distance, the ding of an open car door pounds through my head in a steady allegro, making me grimace. Feet stomp on the pavement in an unnatural beat before being muffled by the grass. A string of questions follows from a deep voice: *Are you alright? Are you hurt? What happened?*

Above us, vehicles whizz by, unaware and oblivious to what happened here nine days ago and what is happening now, just outside of their beams, of their sight.

Their lights fly past us into the dark.

Ángel Mota Berriozábal

Originaire de la ville de Mexico, il a immigré au Canada en 1992. Doctorat en littérature comparée, de l'Université de Montréal. Il a été chroniqueur à la radio CKUT (Montréal), Amisnet (Rome), ainsi qu'à l'émission de télévision Foco Latino, à Montréal. Il a été coéditeur de différentes revues littéraires. Éditeur invité aux éditions Lugar Comun et chez Laberinto Press. Commissaire littéraire de la Fondation LatinArte. Ses poèmes et nouvelles sont publiés dans des magazines et des livres collectifs au Canada, en Espagne, aux États-Unis, au Mexique, en Italie, en France et au Chili. En 2010, il a publié son recueil de nouvelles : *La casa de Nadie y otros relatos*, en 2014 le roman *La confesión en el paraíso*, et en 2017 paraît le livre de poésie érotique : *Un écho de ta voix – Un eco de tu voz*.

Lorsque Chloé sent les outardes

Elle les cherche avec ses yeux, mais ne peut pas les voir. Elle les entendait alors qu'elle traversait l'avenue en route vers le parc. «Elles sont déjà arrivées !» sourit-elle en atteignant le trottoir avec une certaine hâte. Chloé s'arrête et observe le vert intense de l'herbe, oasis au milieu de la ville où il y a des pins rouges, des saules et un certain nombre d'érables. Leur odeur lui est très agréable. «Curieux qu'une volée d'outardes soit ici, au milieu de la ville.» Elle se dirige vers le chemin des pins. Là, elle trouve un étang artificiel où tombent des centaines de feuilles. Elle parvient à voir et à sentir les oiseaux migrateurs. Les outardes marchent maladroitement sur l'herbe, sans se laisser décourager par le froid du début de l'automne. Chloé s'assoit sur un banc, près de l'eau, face aux bipèdes. Elle sourit lorsqu'elle contemple la souplesse de leurs corps et l'originalité de leurs yeux tachetés de blanc. Les outardes s'aventurent près d'elle, sans soucis. L'odeur de leurs corps est celle de l'humidité et des plumes touchées par tous les éléments de la nature.

À la vue des oiseaux, elle se sent secouée par un souvenir d'enfance : elle se voit dans la ville de Val d'Or, en Abitibi. C'est là où elle est née. C'est là aussi où son père travaillait dans l'une des mines d'or. Son oncle Charles, qui avait une chambre dans sa maison, s'enfonçait aussi dans la terre à la recherche de ce trésor, si recherché par le gouvernement. Les autres oncles habitaient une maison près de la sienne, exerçaient le même emploi de misère. Le seul viable. La ville avait un air pollué et fétide où les êtres se levaient tôt pour rentrer sous les pierres et la terre. Des êtres qui se réveillaient à l'aube pour chercher de l'or, travail qui affecterait leurs poumons et alimenterait, chaque jour, le dioxyde de soufre du ciel.

Dans cette ville, Chloé entendait avec grand plaisir les outardes chaque fois qu'elles revenaient au printemps. Car leur retour était l'annonce du dégel, de la mort du froid glacial et de la fin de l'obligation de rester longtemps à la maison. L'arrivée des outardes était le signe que le moment était venu de sortir de la maison et de respirer les parfums de tout ce qui commence à naître, de sortir jouer et de courir sans bottes ni manteaux.

L'arrivée des outardes ne signifiait pas seulement la fin de l'hiver, mais aussi la fin d'une autre année scolaire. Ce qui la rendait nerveuse. L'école était son refuge. Chez elle, que ce fût à la saison froide ou au printemps, l'histoire se répétait toujours. C'est pourquoi elle jouait le plus de temps possible dans la cour, en avant de la maison, ou courait dans les champs avec Line, sa sœur cadette. Et, au moment où le père et l'oncle rentraient du travail, elle s'enfermait dans sa chambre. Ou encore, si Chloé jouait dans le salon, à la vue de son père ou de son oncle, elle sortait immédiatement dans la rue. En compagnie d'autres amies, ou toute seule, elle sautait alors à la corde jusqu'à la tombée de la nuit. C'est dans ces sorties qu'elle l'avait vue pour la première fois : « l'Indienne anichinabée ». C'est par ces mots qu'on la désignait dans le village. Chloé n'a jamais su comment elle s'appelait. « Ils sont tous pareils », disaient les gens de la ville.

La fille anichinabée se rendait tous les jours, seule, à une extrémité de la rue de la maison de Chloé, au loin. De là, elle regardait tout le voisinage. Une fois, elle avait remarqué les cheveux roux de Chloé, les regardant avec curiosité, même avec un certain intérêt. Un jour, il y eut un échange de regards entre les deux : d'une part les yeux verts de Chloé et, de l'autre, ceux de l'Anichinabée, d'un noir intense. Elles échangèrent un sourire timide. Ensuite, l'Anichinabée poursuivit son chemin vers la rivière, comme c'était le cas tous les après-midis. Chloé ne savait pas pourquoi elle se dirigeait toujours là, puisque les maisons des Anichinabés se trouvaient du côté opposé de la ville et, de plus, elle savait que personne dans le quartier où habitaient les Blancs n'aimait voir les Autochtones dans les rues du village.

C'est peut-être pour cette raison que la nuit, alors que Chloé était allongée dans sa chambre, sur un lit à côté de sa sœur Line, et qu'elle entendait, dans la pièce voisine, la poussée frénétique de son père au-dessus de sa mère, elle pensait à l'Anichinabée, à son pas suspect et timoré. Il y avait quelque chose d'astucieux dans son geste et son sourire léger, parce qu'elle marchait comme un renard, toujours sur la défensive et en cachette. Chloé rêvait que la fille Anichinabée marchait sous les peupliers, en route vers la rivière dans laquelle celle-ci immergeait alors tout son corps. Elle la rêvait dans son costume traditionnel, fait de cuir et de perles, avec aux pieds des mocassins en peau de caribou. Elle aimait beaucoup l'odeur du cuir. Chloé voyait comment la fille, une fois dans l'eau, disparaissait, et qu'à sa place une outarde émergeait de la rivière. L'outarde la fixait des yeux comme si elle voulait lui communiquer une parole.

Avec ces rêves, Chloé se réveillait en sueur. La clarté du soleil arrivait par la fenêtre, filtrée par les rideaux. Elle se tournait toujours pour voir sa sœur. Celle-ci dormait. Chloé ressentait de la peur à ce moment-là et elle ne savait pas pourquoi. Une anxiété que seule la clarté du soleil pouvait calmer. Au moment du réveil, en sursaut, que ce fût au printemps ou à l'automne, elle entendait parfois les outardes voler au-dessus de sa maison. Moments où elle se levait du lit à la hâte et s'avançait vers la fenêtre afin d'observer les oiseaux migrateurs, même si la plupart du temps, lorsqu'elle posait les mains sur la vitre, les outardes étaient déjà au loin. Toutefois, dans sa chambre, elle ne cessait de les entendre comme un écho. C'est ainsi que, comme une présence qui nous poursuit, l'image du visage de l'Anichinabée revenait à ses yeux.

Chloé entend dans le parc comment les outardes harcèlent avec fureur les mouettes et les canards, qui se disputent le même étang, en gazouillant de manière continue et en secouant la tête dans tous les sens. L'une des outardes observe de près la femme aux cheveux roux, après s'être approchée d'elle sans crainte. Chloé la fixe, méditative. Elle regarde sa montre et se rend compte qu'elle doit encore attendre une heure avant que sa fille ne sorte de l'école. Elle est reconnaissante de ne pas être obligée d'aller au cégep aujourd'hui pour enseigner la communication, elle peut attendre sa fille à la sortie de l'école, et elle est heureuse de prendre le temps de rédiger quelques notes sur ses recherches avant son voyage au Mexique. Elle jette encore une fois un coup d'œil aux outardes, celles qui marchent avec maladresse autour de son banc. Elle sent leurs excréments, disséminés partout sur l'herbe. Les oiseaux lui ramènent des souvenirs, des images qui l'assaillent tout à coup :

Un matin, elle vit sa mère devant l'évier de la cuisine, comme elle avait l'habitude de le faire tous les jours. Chloé s'assit à la table sans dire un mot, ne voulant rien dire, comme si tout ce qui l'entourait était à éviter. Son oncle Charles dormait. Mais il devait se lever quelques minutes plus tard pour aller à la mine. Son père était déjà là. Voilà pourquoi Chloé se dépêcha de manger un bol de gruau avec du lait. Elle vit le regard anxieux de sa mère, le geste indifférent et fatigué de sa sœur cadette, laquelle avalait cette bouillie d'avoine chaude par gorgées. Dès que l'oncle Charles se lèverait, tout recommencerait à zéro. L'anxiété prit alors tout son sens. Il valait mieux presser le pas et se diriger vers l'école. Ne pas le voir ou l'écouter. On l'entendait cracher dans sa chambre, on l'entendait tousser, une toux qui expulsait de la pierre et de la poussière avalée à cause de son travail dans la mine. Chloé entendit ses pas maladroits sur le plancher de bois. Elle voulut manger en vitesse, et lorsqu'elle s'aperçut de l'augmentation du bruit dans la chambre de son oncle, elle se leva. La mère la regardait de biais, debout devant des œufs brouillés. D'une voix forte, Chloé dit à Line de se hâter. En une minute, elles étaient déjà dans la rue.

Chloé se souvient comment elle s'était réveillée cette nuit-là, tout en sueur. Une fois de plus, elle avait fait un cauchemar. Elle avait rêvé de la fille anichinabée et des outardes. Elle eut peur. Au parc, Chloé se rappelle, en une série d'images discontinues, que ce matin-là elle s'était hâtée de mettre son uniforme. C'était le mois de mai. L'année scolaire toucherait à sa fin dans un mois. Cela signifiait qu'elle resterait, comme toujours, à la maison tout l'été avec son oncle et son père. Chloé se souvint alors qu'elle était allée à la cuisine. Sa mère avait une mine silencieuse, soit par obligation, soit pour éviter de dire un mot. Comme si la réalité de la vie quotidienne lui avait enlevé toute volonté de parler. Elle donnait l'impression de tout faire par instinct ou par habitude, l'habitude de la peur. Chloé se hâta de manger son bol de gruau. L'oncle n'était pas encore levé, bien qu'il fût en retard pour le boulot.

Chloé avait remarqué six bouteilles de bière Molson sur le comptoir de la cuisine, ainsi que des capsules éparpillées sur la table. Elle sentit l'émanation fétide des mégots de cigarettes, écrasés dans le cendrier.

Dans le silence de la cuisine, seulement rompu par le bruit de leurs bouches qui mastiquaient, elle avait entendu de la fenêtre un gazouillement très proche. Elle s'était levée et avait jeté un coup d'œil par la vitre. Elle avait souri avec une joie sans pareil. Son regard était intense et l'expression de son visage exprimait la surprise. Par la fenêtre, elle voyait deux outardes dans le jardin. Celles-ci marchaient d'un pas inquiet, comme si elles craignaient de s'enfoncer plus profondément dans la pelouse, tout en cherchant quelque chose à becqueter, à en juger par leur désir persistant de coller le bec sur l'herbe. Chloé ne pouvait pas bouger, elle ne voulait pas qu'elles partent, elle avait même eu le désir de les caresser, et elle l'aurait fait si ce n'était qu'elles l'auraient mordue ou se seraient envolées. Elle entendait quelques pas lourds et maladroits dans la cuisine ; elle a eu peur. Son visage devint pourpre. Son cœur battait comme une cascade, elle éprouvait une forte anxiété qu'elle contrôlait en restant muette.

– Qu'est-ce que tu fais là, collée à la fenêtre, ostie ? Le ton de la voix de l'oncle était encore lourd de sommeil et marqué d'un malaise causé par la gueule de bois.

Après quelques secondes de silence, ne sachant pas quoi faire ou dire, elle ne pouvait qu'articuler, craintive :

– Il y a deux outardes dans le jardin.

Chloé arrête d'observer les oiseaux dans le parc et prend un livre de Cortázar. Un ami le lui a donné, un ami auquel elle pense maintenant, celui qui lui parle du Mexique, avec qui elle parle souvent de littérature et de ses recherches sur les compagnies minières canadiennes et la destruction de la terre sacrée huichol à San Luis Potosí. «Continuité des parcs» lit-elle, le titre de la première nouvelle du recueil. Elle sourit, méditative. Elle observe à nouveau les outardes qui s'éloignent sur l'eau. Une femme coiffée d'un hidjab arrive au bord de l'eau, tenant sa fille par la main. Elle s'arrête pour prendre des photos, s'adresse en arabe à la petite fille, laquelle reste immobile et souriante devant l'appareil-photo. Chloé regarde à nouveau sa montre. «Est-ce que ma fille va être bien à l'école ? C'est sa première année.»

Un jour, alors qu'elle rentrait de l'école, Chloé se trouva face à une ambulance garée non loin de chez elle. Il y avait des policiers, le bruit de voix stridentes, les gens du voisinage se tenaient debout dans l'entrée de leurs maisons. Elle sentit un pincement au ventre et une peur énorme. Elle courut jusqu'à l'endroit où les gens étaient attroupés. Elle vit sa mère avec son tablier. Dans son visage elle lut une expression horrifiée. Elle se frottait les mains sans relâche. Les Valois, des voisins devant leur maison, commentaient :

– Je l'ai vue passer dans la rue, comme tous les jours. Puis plus rien. Je ne l'aurais jamais imaginé. Elle passait toujours par-là, pointe le voisin de sa main, vers un lieu lointain, près de la rivière.

– On sait ce qui est arrivé, sa conjointe avait l'air agitée, fumant par à-coups. La police ne dit rien, ostie !

Les officiers avaient l'air bête. Chloé s'approcha d'eux, malgré le ruban jaune qu'elle ne devait pas franchir.

– Arrête-toi là, dit le policier aux lunettes noires, en levant la main, d'un geste peu amical.

Chloé réussit à voir les pieds de la fille anichinabée. Elle reconnut ses chaussures et la couleur brune de ses jambes. Le reste du corps, allongé sur la rue, était recouvert d'un plastique noir.

– Un accident ? réussit-elle à articuler avec effroi.

– Non. Dégage. Tu ne peux pas rester ici ! ordonna le policier, sans la regarder. Il fit un geste de la main droite pour l'éloigner.

– La fille anichinabée est devenue une outarde, pensa-t-elle. Elle est allée vers le sud.

– Oui, sûrement les outardes l'ont prise, affirma un homme anichinabé, plus tard du côté des maisons des Nations premières où, par curiosité, Chloé alla faire un tour pour voir où la fille avait vécu. Elle reviendra sous un autre nom. C'est ainsi que va le monde. Et dans ton rêve, tu dis que tu as vu une outarde ? Tu vas la trouver dans le sud, lorsque tu iras. Parce que tu vas y aller un jour, sourit l'Anichinabé.

– Ils l'ont violée trois fois puis l'ont pendue, expliqua la mère à ses enfants, tasse de café à la main, après avoir lu le journal.

– Qui a fait ça, maman ? dit Chloé en tremblant. Son cœur battait plus vite.

– Les policiers ne savent toujours pas. C'est juste une Indienne.

Le sang de Chloé se figea. Elle ressentit de la colère, elle était terrifiée. Elle fut envahie par des sensations qu'elle pensait endormies, reléguées dans l'oubli.

La femme aux cheveux roux, les yeux fixés uniquement sur les lettres du conte de Cortázar, incapable de se concentrer sur le style, se souvient d'elle, montant dans un autocar pour Montréal. Elle se remémore en train de contempler par la vitre du véhicule la forêt boréale qu'elle laissait derrière elle. Chloé évoque, comme quelque chose qui revient sans cesse, le visage de sa mère au moment où elle lui a dit au revoir de la main depuis le quai de la gare routière, en Abitibi. Ce geste de tristesse laissait paraître des pleurs étouffés. La sœur est restée à Val d'Or, mais elle n'avait aucune crainte pour Line. «Elle est ronde. Mon oncle ne la touchera pas. Il aime juste les filles maigres comme moi ou comme l'Anichinabée.»

Chloé pose ses yeux sur les outardes, avec une certaine peur. Elle ne sait pas combien de temps elles resteront là, dans ce parc. «Elles sont juste de passage.» La femme a du mal à poursuivre la lecture de la nouvelle de l'écrivain argentin. Elle laisse le livre *Fin d'un jeu* sur le banc. Elle marche vers les oiseaux migrateurs, en observe un de très près, curieuse. «Bientôt, ma fille sortira de l'école. Aujourd'hui je peux venir, mais j'espère que Pierre viendra la chercher quand je serai au collège. Et puis, les outardes partiront bientôt, et au printemps elles reviendront au parc, comme une continuité. Pour nous, j'espère que ce sera une continuité en transformation. Comme font les outardes que j'entends : elles voyagent par volées sous la forme d'une pointe de flèche, et changent le vol en forme d'écran, en ligne droite ou en cercle, en fonction du vent, à l'unisson pour se protéger les unes et les autres.»

Hugh Hazelton

Hugh is a writer and translator who specializes in the comparison of Canadian and Quebec literatures with those of Latin America, as well as in the work of Latin American writers of Canada. He has written four books of poetry and translates from French, Spanish, and Portuguese into English; his translation of *Vétiver* (Signature, 2005), a book of poems by Joël Des Rosiers, won the Governor General's award for French-English translation in 2006. He is a professor emeritus of Spanish at Concordia University in Montreal and former co-director of the Banff International Literary Translation Centre in Alberta.

Maeve

Maeve, you suddenly appeared so long ago from Uruguay via Argentina Bolivia Peru the Andean Spine to Colombia and a break-up in New Jersey and inexplicably in Montreal for readings of your unflinching always untitled poems about your interior tempests and the world's injustice with sad laconic irony in *Grito con espejo* (*Scream with Mirror*) and *Apenas un caballo* (*Hardly a Horse*), poems like "you're my country/ a diffused warmth/ pretentious sore/ slow asphyxiation of revolvers loaded with words/ I throw myself through the telephone's tube/ suffocate you with pillows of silence/ I face you like a parrot does a train/ without a fuss" that were published and translated and praised as being "the best-kept literary secret in Montreal" and music and parties with people from a dozen countries and conversations over fragrant coffee and your lively or wistful paintings and suddenly your breakdown or crisis or delusions or whatever it was that made you lose control and finally you went off to Caracas to live with your sister Mehedy who played the flute and piccolo in Venezuelan orchestras along with her husband on the violin, where you'd periodically run off and wander into the pungent ranchos on the hills and they'd have to look for you, those stories you'd told me of your mother's instability and your mad but fearless brother who burned through the States and ended up in lush Hawaii where your mother in her eighties flew out to meet him and he rented a sailboat for a week and loaded her onto it in a wheelchair so they could head for California and the Coast Guard stopped them and found her in the musty cabin and towed them back and a decade later you reappeared in Montreal and we met you in the park with our daughter with kids flying kites but you wouldn't come over to the house because we were too happy and you lived in small apartments in Côte-des-Neiges and said you'd finally calmed your mind just as your body started to give out as you finished the manuscript of the anguished maelstrom poems of manuelmadre and your legs slowly weakened and you'd come to the readings with a cane, then a walker and finally you ended up in a wheelchair in a flat for people with disabilities and could only go out if someone pushed you down and up the ramp and along the sidewalk and fewer and fewer friends would visit because your cigarette smoke was so chokingly thick and in the winter we couldn't take you outside at all but you'd talk on the phone endlessly with Ginette when she had cancer and couldn't go out herself and you taught her Spanish with a Río de la Plata accent so she'd say, "Hola Maeve," and then she passed away and after that you and I would talk, and one day your hospital called me and asked if I could come quickly because the doctor wanted to perform further tests on your lungs because there was a cloud in one and you refused and when I got there he said, "I'll give you three minutes," and I spoke to you about Ginette and her struggle and acceptance and you finally said yes and I went with you every week in adapted transport for your tests and we got the final results and they sent you to antiseptic palliative care where a kindly woman explained what was to come and then asked, "Who's your caregiver here?" and the three of us realized it was me, and you called Mehedy in Venezuela and the doctor wrote a letter of extreme emergency to the Embassy there requesting a visa and three days later Mehedy arrived to care for you as she did in Caracas and we talked and joked and recalled things and looked at your paintings and sketches that Mehedy brought from your apartment and then things got worse and they put you into a coma in a plastic tent because the pain was going to be too horrible and the next day you suddenly came to and looked at me and said, "Hugo," as you always did and cried with your sister and then they gave you an injection and you died that night, and a few days later, as you wished, Mehedy and I and your friend Luz Vida and the two social workers who'd looked after you for a decade took your ashes on a fragrant spring morning to the footbridge by the old mill in the park on Île-de-la-Visitation and let your ashes slip away into the Rivière-des-Prairies as we silently said goodbye and Mehedy played the flute and an oriole on a branch above the river suddenly stopped singing.

Elvira Truglia

Elvira Truglia has worked in the non-profit sector for many years, focusing on policy, communications, education, and program management to advance social inclusion, community development, and human rights. In parallel, she is a writer and journalist covering the intersections of culture, politics, and social issues. She has written for media outlets like the *Huffington Post*, *Rabble.ca*, *New Canadian Media*, as well as literary magazines and communications journals. Her broadcast work has aired on Canada's CBC Radio, the US-based social justice radio program, *Making Contact*, and independent/community media networks, locally and internationally. She recently co-hosted/produced *The Traffik Report*, a podcast on human trafficking in Canada. A multimedia storyteller, Elvira's documentary photos were featured in *Points of View*, a national human rights photography exhibition at the Canadian Museum for Human Rights. Whether writing, working on a media project, or advocating for social change, Elvira is humbled by the power of nature and the human spirit.

The Smell of Joy

There it is. The whiff of sweet vanilla. I knew it was there; I was following it like a golden retriever tracks scent. I used to love that smell as a child but now it spirals me into a catch-me-if-you-can chase for fragrance.

I find it hiding inside an ornament on the coffee table. The offending smell comes from a burnt baby blue candle, dotted with fading yellow stars. It was my sister's. A gift she received more than twenty years ago. My mom has a knack for throwing away heirlooms, like handwritten letters from nonna that marked my mother's migration from Southern Italy. Yet she keeps random things, like scented candles connected to our childhood.

I love going to Ottawa to visit my family for Christmas, but it always comes with hesitation. I often get heart palpitations, shortness of breath, nausea, headaches, brain fog, chills, and/or tinnitus after being exposed to a fragrance or something in the air. This time, it is thanks to the perfumed candle. The fine particles—felt but not seen—throw my nervous system off balance.

I owe this reaction to environmental sensitivities/multiple chemical sensitivity, a condition that makes me intolerant to smoke, fragrance, indoor chemicals, outdoor pollutants, or even the lingering unidentifiable smell on my daughter's school clothes—basically, most things people are exposed to daily.

My mom tries hard to understand what happens to me after an exposure, such as being close to the vanilla scented candle, but it's beyond her. If you detect things that go unnoticed by the average non-sensitive person, you are always faced with the choice of disclosure or avoidance. If I tell her, she responds with either guilt, dismissal, frustration, or denial. Avoidance is the easier path—find the source, remove it if you can, or physically remove yourself.

It often gets awkward. One time in 1998, I decided to visit friends in Vancouver for New Year's. I arrived at my friend's high-rise condo and wanted to run right back out the door almost immediately. My body could feel the invisible volatile organic compounds (VOCs) (like formaldehyde) in the air. They were coming from laminate flooring, baseboards, kitchen cupboards, furniture—anything that was made from composite wood products (wood scraps and waste that are melded together with glue). Chemicals, like VOCs, are ubiquitous and are associated with long-term health risks, including cancer. For sensitives like me, off-gassing VOCs have an immediate impact—they make finding a safe space to live or visit almost impossible. I was grateful that my host offered me a place to stay for the week, yet I could barely stay for one night. I sat in the guest room, intent on practicing mind over matter (*I'm safe, I'm grateful to be here, I'm safe, I am grateful to be here*). But trying to use positive affirmations to override my physical symptoms didn't make them go away. My only choice was to leave.

In time, I learned to get used to these awkward moments. I had to because they began to multiply, especially in my newly adopted city. I moved from Ottawa to Montreal in 1996, two years before Quebec introduced the Tobacco Act, restricting the use of tobacco in workplaces. With a new job as editor of an international community radio magazine, I would have to bear the smell of second- and third-hand smoke for a while as colleagues in our shared office space struggled to get used to going downstairs to smoke rather than lighting up at their desk.

Our building was on St. Laurent Blvd., an artery crossing the geographic heart of the city from north to south. Also referred to as The Main, the boulevard was a gateway to working class neighbourhoods and mom and pop shops established by immigrants in the twentieth century. By the '90s, The Main was thriving as a trendy haven for artists who could find cheap rent and good eats. The road also divided the city's two solitudes—the French-speaking community to its east, the English-speaking community to the west. Working on The Main seemed like the perfect welcome to the cultural and political history of the city. This immersion gave me a small taste of what my parents might have felt as newcomers trying to navigate their place in a completely new environment.

A few months after I started my new job, the smoke situation at the office started to get better until the perfume assault began. A new administrative assistant joined the team. Her reception desk was a few metres down the hallway from the office entrance, guaranteeing exposure to her signature scent, a floral musky concoction worn as an accessory to her tailored skirt suits from Paris. My tightened airways and recently diagnosed asthma helped me advocate and request a fragrance-free workspace. At the time, perfume was already known to cause respiratory issues for some people, although its connection to neurotoxins (phthalates, synthetic musks, and sensitizers), hormone imbalance, and cancer were still emerging.

I worked with a multicultural crew from Senegal, Colombia, France, and Quebec. In this crowd, my request for a fragrance-free office was seen as demanding, "Canadian," and unusual. There was some mild empathy from my boss, who talked with the admin assistant about her perfume. After that, I had to endure looks of disdain from my musk-scented colleague born at the epicentre of European perfume production (France). My health needs disrupted the centuries-long branding of perfume as a sign of luxury, beauty, and class. Still, I understood why fragrance marketing is so powerful. Scent is the only of our five senses that goes directly to the limbic system, which connects to the memory and emotional centres of the brain. In my colleague's case, wearing perfume was likely not just a daily routine but a habit that connected her to memories of home. Two realities co-existed; fragrance propelled one of us to feel safe and the other to run away looking for a safe harbour because of MCS.

Multiple chemical sensitivity (MCS) is a medical condition characterized by adverse health effects from exposure to common chemicals and pollutants. As of 2020, more than 1.1 million Canadians had been diagnosed with MCS, a 41% increase from 2010 levels. According to Statistics Canada, 3.5% of the Canadian population, mostly women, suffer from MCS.

But Canadians are not alone. MCS is a global phenomenon. Prevalence of MCS in several European countries, Japan, and the US appears in research studies, and there are also reports of MCS in Mexico, Brazil, Korea, Vietnam, Trinidad and Tobago, and Ecuador. MCS affects more than 61 million people across just the US, UK, Sweden, and Australia.

Despite millions of people around the world experiencing similar symptoms from environmental exposures, the illness is marred with social stigma and controversy. Conditions that don't fit conventional medical paradigms of biological cause and effect are considered idiopathic, or of unknown origin. This is true for fibromyalgia, chronic fatigue syndrome, and other complex chronic illnesses like MCS that are on the rise.

Conventional biomedicine is founded on the separation of body and mind. If biomarkers (considered objective medical signs) cannot be found to explain symptoms then the causes are considered unknown and are assumed to be mind-based (psychiatric or psychosomatic). In the past, epilepsy, migraine, Alzheimer's, and asthma were once considered disorders of unknown origin until biomarkers were found. Despite research explaining the mechanisms of MCS, it often continues to be labelled as psychogenic. The result is stigma, social isolation, poverty along with the lack of appropriate health care, housing and workplace accommodation.

As my boss and I got to know each other better, we became friends. She had a soft spot for me (and vice versa) but, like most, she didn't understand my MCS. Speaking to me like an older sister dishing out tough love, she gave me a perspective check: "*I guess you'll end up living like a hermit on a mountain because it's the only way you will be able to get away from perfume, cigarettes, and other things that bother you.*" She hit a nerve. I didn't want to be isolated from people. I came to Montreal to be in the metropolis, explore my creativity, my identity, and make my world more expansive. I came to Montreal to do my Master's in Media Studies. I was writing a radio drama about identity politics in the city with the second-largest population of Italian-Canadians. I had so many questions. I wanted to see what it meant to be in a place where people proudly wore their ethnicity on their sleeves rather than something to hide or put on parade on designated days (like in Ottawa). But my boss's words warned me of how small my world could become. I was determined to find a way to beat this, or at least learn to live with it.

What I didn't realize at the time is that there are fates worse than living like a hermit in nature. As I became more involved in the growing environmental illness community, I began to hear about people who ended up living in their cars in the middle of nowhere to get away from urban exposures and unsuitable housing. In February 2022, there were news stories about "Sophia," who went through with medically assisted dying. She spent years seeking suitable and affordable housing—free of smoke, fragrances, and VOCs—to no avail. Since Canada's medical assistance in dying law now considers applications from people whose death cannot be reasonably foreseen, several people with MCS have sought and received medically-assisted death as a remedy for unbearable suffering.

But back to the early 2000s, when my life of discovery in Montreal continued. I finished my radio drama, graduated, got married, had a baby girl and my MCS kept getting worse.

In 2011, I landed a job with a non-profit focused on empowering girls and young women. It was in the already waning cultural hub of the city, an area dotted with industrial buildings converted into residential and commercial spaces. Our open-air loft was known as the beehive; three rows of workspaces were surrounded by stacked windows that streamed natural light on two sides of the office. It was hipster heaven except for the off-gassing from constant building renovations by new tenants reconfiguring their spaces, adding walls, paint, doors, or who resanded and varnished wood floors. This would often happen without advance notice. The result was brain fog, dizziness, difficulty breathing, nausea, and a sprint to hastily pack up my belongings, leave the building, and hope to recover enough to work from home.

One day, a new communications officer sent me an article on environmental sensitivities. I finally felt seen as I read about other people like me, who had similar stories. I recognized one of the names in the article, Sonia Di Capo, and decided to reach out.

I found out that Sonia had become chemically-sensitive from mould exposure. Many years of living in an apartment with black mould behind her bedroom walls left her sick. She had a series of chronic conditions: MCS, mould illness, chronic fatigue syndrome, various infections. Her struggle for survival was relentless. Even after her apartment was remediated, she continued to live with debilitating conditions that left her unable to work but determined to find help.

Deep diving into research on mould, she discovered the world of functional medicine and started following protocols to detox and support her immune system. This holistic approach to managing chronic disease involves a lot of trial and error. When we met in person or spoke on the phone, Sonia was eager to share her research, the treatments she discovered, and names of doctors and functional medicine practitioners. Sonia was doing everything she could to get out of survival mode.

Eventually, she left her beloved city of Montreal to live in St. Adele, a picturesque town in the Laurentian Mountains. I asked her about driving along the mountain highway towards St. Adele. She said she knew she was getting close when the mountain air became palpable, and the hold of her brain fog started to let go. "It's incredible," she said.

***

In 2015, I met Lisa Edelsward at an event organized by the Environmental Health Association of Quebec, a group that advocates and raises public awareness about MCS. For over three decades, Lisa had been living with environmental illness. During that time, she also developed chronic fatigue syndrome (ME/CFS) and faced a perfect storm of overlapping chronic conditions that were little understood. She tried living in Ottawa and the outskirts of Montreal, but it was never "good enough." Symptoms would rise and wane and rise again. Her research into locations with pristine air quality led her to a new home on the Pacific Coast, in Sooke, British Columbia. When I met Lisa, she divided her time between Montreal and Sooke, based on her husband's teaching schedule at Montreal's premiere university.

Her apartment in Montreal was strategically chosen for the proximity and view of the city's emblematic landmark, Mount Royal. The Mountain became a park in 1876 and has served as a refuge to city dwellers ever since. It is home to mammals, amphibians, reptiles, birds, more than seven hundred plant species, and ninety species of trees.

On a beautiful fall day, I met up with Lisa for a hike on Mount Royal. One of the best ways to access the park is walking to the end of Peel Street and climbing the Peel steps all the way to the top for a view of the city, the St. Lawrence River, and on a clear day, even Vermont. You can stop along the way to explore the meandering pathways in the woods. As we worked our way up, my breath got shorter, but Lisa's remained steady, a stamina she built from daily trips to the Mountain. With each breath, we inhaled the smell of birch and maple trees. Decomposing leaves were starting to turn orange, yellow, and red, and left the unmistakable earthy sweet smell of fall. For Lisa, the forest evoked the "smell of joy" and I knew exactly what she meant.

Sometimes, when I am on a hike like that one, I remember the trails of the mountain I walked along in my childhood. When I was a toddler, I followed my nonna on the hills of the Calabrian countryside blooming with lavender, wild oregano, fennel, and olive trees spilling over steep, winding paths that led to her garden. For me, those hills were filled with smells of joy.

Always curious, I wondered why it always feels so good to be on a mountain. I found out there is a scientific reason behind the joy. Negative ions found in forests release serotonin (the happy hormone) and make us feel better. The negative ions also work on a cellular level—acting as antioxidants to allow our bodies to achieve equilibrium.

This also explains the lifting brain fog that Sonia described when she hit the Laurentian mountains. Things were starting to click. Sonia moved to the mountains; Lisa sought refuge in the mountains.

Between my life experience and the experiences people shared with me, I couldn't get out my head, what my colleague said to me in 1998: *The only way you will be able to stay away from pollutants is to live like a hermit on a mountain.* It was clear my boss was telling me that if I wanted to live in today's world, I would have to get a grip and deal with exposures.

And I have been trying to do that—I tell myself to just get out there and enjoy the city. After all, I live in one of the most coveted neighbourhoods in Montreal—Little Italy. With its overflow of restaurants, coffee shops, the largest outdoor market in North America, village-like feel, and dozens of winding alleyways that become makeshift parks in all seasons, it's a destination for tourists, long-standing and gentrified residents alike. Grateful to be in such a dynamic place, I tell myself that the green alleyways will be my urban refuge. Many are lined with trees, plants, and even bird houses. So, I get out there with my dog, rain or shine. But inevitably, especially on humid summer days, the wafting cigarette, weed, or barbeque smoke combines with the toxic detergent and dryer sheet steam spewing out of laundry vents and takes an oppressive toll. The brain fog kicks in, so does the asthma, and it's back indoors, windows shut to avoid the same scents from drifting in. I have become a hermit, but not on a mountain, in my own neighbourhood.

This is why I can't seem to heed my old boss's message to just get a grip—because I actually can't deal with the exposures. Environmental pollutants, fragrance, and toxic building materials are everywhere. They have become so normalized that people like me who cannot tolerate them are considered unsuitable for the modern world. Dramatic pause. But is the modern world really normal?

I have been asking that question for a long time and recently picked up Gabor Maté's latest book, *The Myth of Normal: Trauma, Illness and Healing in a Toxic Culture.* One of the key ideas the renowned Canadian doctor and author develops in his book is that we assume society is living in healthy or "normal" conditions simply because we're used to them, even when they're not healthy at all.

He says disease is a way of adapting to abnormal circumstances.

Same goes for the external environment. Since 2008, the mountain where Lisa and I sought refuge has been feeling the wrath of the emerald ash borer, an unwelcome beetle that destroys ash trees and threatens biodiversity. All thanks to climate change—human-made abnormal circumstances that happen to be the greatest threat to our existence on the planet. The mountain has been trying to adapt to its new circumstances. It is a symbol of resilience. After all, not all the ash trees have succumbed to the ash borer and even after terrible ice storms like the one in 1998, the mountain adapts, it rebuilds (with the help of city intervention).

So maybe I just need to learn to be more resilient. After all, the fragility of the mountain's ecosystem mirrors our own. We, too, are facing foreign invaders, a barrage of chemicals and pollutants that assault people with environmental illness every day. Still, our bodies are struggling to adapt to the upheaval that just keeps coming. Why is it so hard?

Always searching for answers, I look to the research. Reacting to unusually low levels of chemicals questions conventional wisdom that the "dose makes the poison." This basic principle of toxicology says that the amount of exposure to chemicals determines how dangerous or toxic they are to human health. But what if it's not just about how much you are exposed to, but the nature of the chemicals, when you were exposed, for how long, how much you already have in your system (bioaccumulation), genetic factors and interactions of all the above that determines toxicity? If this is true, the foundational understanding of biology and disease is put into question. And this is exactly what is happening. In other words, what's changed is scientific understanding about how much we can be exposed to before getting sick.

Another thing that has changed is the sheer volume of chemicals and their nature. There is now a class of manufactured chemicals called forever chemicals (such as PFAS) that stay in the environment and our bodies forever and accumulate over time. There are 350,000 types of synthetic chemicals in our ecosystem, including pesticides, plastics, antibiotics, and industrial chemicals. There are five times as many manufactured chemicals as there were in 1950, and the number is expected to triple by 2050.

This is huge. We have gone over a threshold that keeps the ecosystem in balance and humans safe because we globally can't keep up with the rate at which chemicals are being produced. We have reached the tipping point.

This chronic exposure accumulates in the body to create a toxic load that triggers chronic inflammation and is a catalyst for disease.

After years of deep diving on environmental illness and looking at myself like a research project, I think I have found the reason people like me have a hard time—our systems are simply overloaded. One of my go-to sources is Dr. Molot who, over three decades, has treated more than 12,000 patients with environmentally-linked illnesses. In his book, *12,000 Canaries Can't Be Wrong*, he traces the impact of environmental pollutants to explain multiple chemical sensitivity.

Dr. Molot says there is plenty of evidence that MCS is a "distinct biological entity" pointing to genetics that make it difficult to detox, the accumulation of oxidative stress from environmental exposures, and brain receptors that are activated or sensitized to detect environmental stimuli (TRPVI receptors).

Despite evidence pointing to root causes of MCS, the debate about MCS still lingers. Why? Think back to what is considered normal. Chemicals are so pervasive that they are normalized. They are just considered part of the modern world.

But Maté argues that it's time to stop ignoring the status quo. He says we need to pay attention to the signs of a toxic culture that are making us sick. There is an epidemic of chronic illness, which affects women and other vulnerable communities disproportionately. MCS is just one example. I say we also need to pay attention to the signs of a toxic environment. People with MCS are signs. They are the canaries in the proverbial coal mine, warning others that environmental exposures, our modern lives, are making us sick. We need to rethink normal.

Maybe this is how I can explain the need to avoid the vanilla scented candle to my mom without feeling like a burden. Maybe, like Gabor Maté says, my response to abnormal circumstances is, in fact, normal. Maybe my ability to sense things others can't is a superpower that can help others, like a canary in the coalmine.

Suddenly, going to the mountain has new meaning. Maybe it isn't a life sentence of isolation but a path to healing, a metaphor for the paradigm shift we need. Sonia, Lisa, and others I met have climbed the mountain. They have left the city, are practicing avoidance, are reclaiming their lives in nature. They are defining their own normal.

I am still searching, but not for the blue candle with yellow stars at my mom and dad's house; that search will always lead me to the same place. Instead, as I continue to learn more about MCS, its roots and paths to healing, I will no longer resist the mountain, I will embrace it and welcome the smell of joy.

References

"Body Burden: The Pollution in Newborns." *Environmental Working Group*, 14 July 2005, www. ewg.org/research/body-burden-pollution-newborns.

Carnahan, Jill. "Shining Light on a Mysterious Illness: Multiple Chemical Sensitivity." *Dr. Jill Carnahan, MD*, 16 July 2019, www.jillcarnahan.com/2018/08/10/shining-light-on-a-mysterious-illness-multiple-chemical-sensitivity/. Accessed 10 Aug. 2023.

"Cheatsheet: Volatile Organic Compounds." *Environmental Working Group*, 14 May 2008, www. ewg.org/news-insights/news/cheatsheet-volatile-organic-compounds. Accessed 10 Aug. 2023.

"Chemical Pollution Has Passed Safe Limit for Humanity, Say Scientists." *The Guardian*, 18 Jan. 2022, www.theguardian.com/environment/2022/jan/18/chemical-pollution-has-passed-safe-limit-for-humanity-say-scientists. Accessed 10 Aug. 2023.

del Valle, Elena. "Scent Marketing Connects to Hispanics on a Deep Cultural Level." *Hispanic Marketing & Public Relations Website and Podcast*, 13 Sept. 2011, hispanicmpr.com/ resources/old-articles/scent-marketing-connects-to-hispanics-on-a-deep-cultural-level/. Accessed 10 Aug. 2023.

Maté, Gabor, and Daniel Maté. *The Myth of Normal: Trauma, Illness and Healing in a Toxic Culture.* Knopf Canada, 2022.

Molot, John, et al. "Multiple Chemical Sensitivity: It's Time to Catch up to the Science." *Neuroscience & Biobehavioral Reviews*, vol. 151, 2023, p. 105227, https://doi. org/10.1016/j.neubiorev.2023.105227.

Molot, John. *12,000 Canaries Can't Be Wrong: Establishing the New Era of Environmental Medicine.* EnviroHealth Publications, 2013.

Pinkas, Adi, et al. "Neurotoxicity of Fragrance Compounds: A Review." *Environmental Research*, vol. 158, 2017, pp. 342–349, https://doi.org/10.1016/j.envres.2017.06.035.

"SQ 1998, C 33 | Tobacco Act | Canlii." www.canlii.org/en/qc/laws/astat/sq-1998-c-33/latest/ sq-1998-c-33.html. Accessed 10 Aug. 2023.

Stein, Eleanor. "Multiple Chemical Sensitivity and Anxiety: Dispelling the Myth." *Is Multiple Chemical Sensitivities Real? | By Dr. Eleanor Stein*, 28 June 2022, www. eleanorsteinmd.ca/blog/multiple-chemical-sensitivity-and-anxiety. Accessed 10 Aug. 2023.

Steinemann, Anne. "International Prevalence of Chemical Sensitivity, Co-Prevalences with Asthma and Autism, and Effects from Fragranced Consumer Products." *Air Quality, Atmosphere & Health*, vol. 12, no. 5, 2019, pp. 519–527, https://doi. org/10.1007/s11869-019-00672-1.

Steinemann, Anne. "National Prevalence and Effects of Multiple Chemical Sensitivities." *Journal of Occupational & Environmental Medicine*, vol. 60, no. 3, 2018, https://doi. org/10.1097/jom.0000000000001272.

Verville, Marie-Hélène. "Malades Pour Vrai." *Gazette Des Femmes*, 13 Mar. 2020, gazettedesfemmes.ca/6376/malades-pour-vrai/. Accessed 10 Aug. 2023.

Dafne Romero

Dafne was born in Mexico City. He migrated to Montreal when he was nineteen years old. He has been a freelance filmmaker for twenty-five years. Dafne worked as producer, director, photographer, editor, and curator in various organizations including universities across Canada and has published poetry. He is working on his first film fiction script. Dafne is an active citizen scientist focused on Kelp Forest. He is the owner of NPK Wild Foods Inc., a kelp company founded in 2009. Dafne harvests and develops kelp products for human consumption and bio stimulants for agriculture, and does research for kelp restoration. In addition, he is an active scuba diver, sailor, and wild forager. Dafne identifies as transgender, and he loves tree climbing.

A Wild Day

It's six o'clock on an icy spring morning. My Highlander Carrier vessel is ready for Pepe and I to embark on a West Coast adventure. Cruising in the west narrows is truly an epic experience. Schools of fish make swirling patterns on the ocean's surface. If I'm attentive, I can hear the liquid whispers of their movements. The venerable black bear on shore digs its furry paws into the sand to feast on hermit crabs, barnacles, limpets, and mussels. When the tide is low, the intertidal zone is exposed, revealing so many magnificent sea animals. The smell changes when this happens; it's a multilayered smell of sand and crustaceans, as well as the occasional stench of dead fish. The pelagic birds bring beauty to those smelly moments, and my nose adapts quickly to the occasion.

A flock of cormorants stand on islets with their wings spread, drying their wet feathers so they can fly again. When those intimate moments happen, I slow down, and I observe. Soon, the current takes control of my boat's direction and the vapour from the Salicornia tapestry on the mud dunes takes over my nostrils. My olfactory nerves try to differentiate that peculiar musky aroma from the glasswort; the scent of this ancient halophyte always tricks me. When burned, glasswort becomes soda ash, which is essential to glass making. In Haida Gwaii, we call it sea asparagus. When I first encountered sea asparagus while foraging, I was mesmerized by its prehistoric look. Especially in September, when the tips start turning magenta while the stem below remains green; then I know autumn is here.

My method of harvesting Salicornia is to grab the bundle with my left hand and, with my right, cut above the stem's basal area. If I harvest at low tide, I get a whiff of the salt marsh's perfume. The green and salty clay odours open my pores and cleanse my skin. I bring a handful on board with the intention of making a wild salad. Savouring the crunchy salty taste as I harvest, I learned they are best in early summer, before or after they become woody, dried, and bitter. I steam the Salicornia, add truffle oil, squeeze a thick slice of bergamot orange, and grind red and green peppercorn on top. I prepare this succulent salad every time I can, varying the ingredients according to the season. It is part of my seasonal food source. I call this meal Pacific Samphire Salad.

When I breathe in the West Coast, my soul is fed on beauty and ambrosia. In saline environments like this, I feel a profound vibration in my chest. The terpenes from Sitka spruce trees, the sweet smell from long stretches of Laminaria Saccharina, better known as sugar kelp, are defining moments in this fine day that I want to share with the world. I anchor the Highlander Carrier at the entrance to Chaatl Island. The sparkling sunny day reflects the grandiose mountain range of Graham and Moresby Islands.

Today, in the strong and relentless Skidegate Channel there is not a single ripple of water. A very enticing day for snorkeling. I make a spontaneous decision to put on my wetsuit, fins, booties, mask, and I jump overboard. The cold water on my face awakens my fascination for the Pacific reefs and marine life. The bounty of life under water is infinite and the iridescent colours evoke imaginary smells in my mind. The bull kelp mermaids caress my whole body and I'm overtaken by their sensual moves; its curvy dance is irresistibly contemplative and seduces me to the point that I forget to breathe. It's extremely addicting to spend time underwater, admiring the beauty of it all. Palmaria delicately dances, flashing metallic burgundy. Ulva's charming emerald greens. The kelp canopy's refined red browns and bronze. The watermelon pink corallines on the rocks. The myriad of hues keeps my mind away from black and white thinking. It is humbling. Every second below the surface is priceless.

Soon enough, my lungs force me to rush up the surface to grab some air and, as I take in the intense scent of rotting wood floating on the surface, my romantic moment brusquely comes to a halt. I refuse to stay in that state of mind and when I take in another deep breath, I recognize the familiar ochre aroma of the giant kelp forest. It is close by! This inevitable trace relaxes my body and I let myself go, floating on cerulean waters mirroring cloud formations on my pupils. My nares pulsate like fish gills, seeking to identify the scent of nebulosus clouds. I feel the chill in my hands and my inebriated state dissipates. It is time to return on board and to dry out. The tides are coming in and the waves are building as I climb the boat ladder. Pepe is happy to see me and wags his tail.

The ice carpets on the edge of the shore are gone and the morning no longer burns my face as I navigate throughout the rugged West Coast. I pour hot coffee into my cup, taking the pleasant aroma of toasted nuts, reminding me that I am still enjoying the morning wonders of nature and there is time to harvest some wild sugar kelp. This fascinating brown kelp is Saccharina Latissima, a cold-water seaweed. Sugar kelp form perfect nooks for hundreds of shore animals and the red turban limpets, blue top snails, and idotea isopod feed on Laminaria blades, which can extend up to three meters. It is delightful to witness the dense population of shell life that lives on Laminaria's canopy. When I simmer kombu blades into a broth, I lean over and wave the evaporating sugary scent into my face.

The icy morning is gone, like a sudden smell—a little reminder that each moment is unique, with its own fragrance. I inhale the ocean and see floating transects of pollen as I navigate throughout Skidegate Channel. The pollen lines are marking rugged shores. It's a great joy to know spring tide is right in my face. The smells of spruce flora from the resin drops on the bark. My sensory neurons recognize the young, scaly spruce cones. The greenery of citric fragrances refreshes the mid-morning, triggering a childhood memory of the sweet scent of pineapple. While the ocean crashes on the rocks, the bivalves reek. Meanwhile, corallines and rhodophyte's seaweeds glitter. After two hours of navigating this splendid environment, my face red from the cold, I crave red seaweed with its taste of bacon! It's incredible how red seaweed resembles bacon and umami, particularly palmaria. When toasted with coconut butter, my palate and olfactory senses cannot distinguish between bacon or palmaria.

It's already late afternoon, time to gather some driftwood and start a nice hot fire for dinner. Pepe chases deer into the lush second growth forest and catches the smell of black bear. He knows very well when one is nearby. I depend on his power of smell, and it never fails. As I gather wood on the shore, I stumble on a myriad of agate, and everything slows down. I hold an agate in my palm and deeply inhale the peculiar dimethyl perfume of the beach. My nasal passages are wide open to receive the wet smell, triggering an image of heavy rainfall in my limbic system. I feel a bit cold. The coastal vegetation creates a symphony of scent. Pepe starts getting high from it; he runs endlessly, chasing smells while I am mesmerized, remembering the Byzantine vases carved out of these gems. I forget my mission to collect firewood as I smell the presence of a nearby ancient Haida village. We are close to Chaatl's totem pole, and I reflect on how Haida art is linked to the underwater world, whereas those that I carry from my Mexican ancestry are tied to celestial deities. The oval shapes of utilitarian objects are like water drops. Decorative art made of argillite features sockeye curves and dorsal fin shapes. Haida potlatch smells of K'aaw, a dish of crunchy and fishy herring roe on kelp, steamed in ocean water and mixed with butter and soya sauce. Bittersweet moieties that can only be remembered by the odours of colonial wars and famine.

The chilly noon tide brings me back to the present moment. All is calm and still, the tips of the trees creaking as they move with strong winds. The tides are changing; the water levels reach my steps, polishing jaspers as the water moves back and forward into the coastline. Pepe barks loudly and hides between my legs, preventing me from walking forward. A bear has found our animal smell and is coming to investigate. He silently appears out of the forest, walking slowly toward us, moving his nostrils and shaking his sharp face side to side. My heart beats like a chainsaw. At this moment, I wish I were odourless. Pepe doesn't stop barking. My body is frozen. We clearly know there isn't any chance for us to run away from this encounter. My sweat probably fills its nose as it continues to walk in our direction. Now we are one metre away from the bear. I smell my pee and feel the hot liquid falling down my legs as I grab Pepe's furry neck and close his jaw with my hand. He gets it! And is quietly growling. The bear stops and looks at me with its small aubergine eyes. I turn away from their regard and start chanting indescribable words of fear. I can smell my own fear, a combination of testosterone and sweat. My whole body trembles with the terrifying image of being eaten alive. I gently pet Pepe's torso. The bear walks away, probably repulsed by our pestilence. I keep chanting as I watch the bear go; salty tears wet my face. I am a total mess. I don't know how much time has passed since the bear left. Pepe is trying to follow the bear path, slowly, with his tail between his legs, carefully sniffing every centimetre of the wild beast's footprints.

I recover and rapidly gather wood and cedar bark. I go back to the vessel and grab my knife and a spool of hemp string. I meticulously make cedar bundles to smudge the space, thanking the bear for peacefully walking away from us. With my right hand, I grab the tip of a cedar branch covered with leafless shrub lichen. Usnea has beautiful fungi structures, pale grey and green hairy-looking webs. Its light body clings to tree branches like stalactites. I stretch to grab a few of them and put them in my pocket. I scratch the floral sap wound from the spruce and collect the bark fallen on the tree root system. Now I need hand-sized rocks to make a circle around the area designated for my fire pit.

The smell of my pee and sweat makes me nauseous. I go to the vessel and take off my clothes. I can't stand the smell anymore. I bravely jump into the ocean and scream from the cold shock to my body. I swim as fast as I can back to shore, my naked body shivering. Pepe watches my painful moments. I quickly run back to the vessel and grab the sap wrapped in usnea from my stinky pants, a lighter from the wheelhouse, a flat iron pan and old stove grills from a metal box where I store camping items. I put on dry clothes. My feet are purple, numb and my nipples hard as pinecones. I make a bunch of wood shavings. The fire is going, and Pepe is busy digging in the tide line, splashing sea water into his face. He tries to catch the hermit crabs that run fast to escape his sharp claws. The hot crack from the incandescent pile of burned wood expels warm wind and my sense of safety is restored. I calm myself down. The sour smell dissipates, and my heart is beating at a normal speed.

Foraging is grounding. I bushwhack, looking for cantharellus, boletus or polyozellus. Soon enough, a dark blue frond appears at the base of a giant spruce. I scan the circumference of this gorgeous mushroom cluster. My mushroom hunting instincts are in full force when I find Golden Pacific chanterelles. Pepe jumps through mountains of fallen branches, also crazy from the mushroom smells all over his snout. I inhale boletus edulis! I see the spongy beige cap and voluptuous white stem standing right beside a second growth hemlock. What a treat. Now, a quest for juniper berries for my wild feast. The resinous aroma becomes stronger as I go deeper into the forest. Labrador shows up everywhere, a stunning low-growing shrub with smooth olive-green leaves with fuzzy white on the underside. Its exquisite rhododendron smells welcome us to the bog, a wetland ecosystem of peat-rich soil and sphagnum dunes. 400-million-year-old lichens show up in the form of foliose on barks. Branchy grey reindeer lichen is a crucial food source for caribou. Little trumpets seem to extend from the cup lichen while light green beard lichen grows from old growth evergreens.

Pepe's underbody is covered in mud and his head is completely sunk in the moss, sniffing thousands of boggy scents. I grab juniper berries. I can't resist eating them right away. The piney smell combined with the musty hints is glamorous to my brain and palette. Pepe is hysterical with the ambrosia. Our ectasis reaches the highest peaks. A timeless afternoon. I head back to shore and use my shirt as a bag to carry all the wild food we gathered. Pepe's head is still hidden in the moss banks and juniper bushes. I am drunk from all the aromas mixed with the berry's flavours.

The fire pit is dim now, but luckily still burning. I put the grill down and place the iron pan on top. I slice the blue mushrooms and the porcini and toss them in the pan; the water evaporates, and the porcini turns purple. I steam the samphire and use the salty water to boil the seashell pasta. I grab my lunch box and cut a thick chunk of butter, add it to the mushrooms, and sprinkle mini kelp flakes and crushed multi-coloured peppercorns. I drop a few tablespoons of truffle oil and squeeze an orange into the glasswort salad. Dinner is ready. Another wild day for Pepe and me, full of memories.

Kelly Kaur

Kelly grew up in Singapore and lives in Calgary, Canada. Her novel, *Letters to Singapore* was launched in Canada and at Asia's Ubud Writers Festival in Bali, Indonesia. Her works have been published internationally: *Understorey Magazine*, Blindman Session Beer Cans, *Best Asian Stories 2020*, *Let in the Light Anthology*, Asia, *Best Asian Poetry 2021-2022*, International Human Rights Arts Festival, New York (2021 and 2022), *Growing Up Indian* (Singapore 2022), The North Dakota Human Rights Arts Festival Travelling Exhibition 2022 and 2023, and *Landed: Transformative Stories of Canadian Immigrant Women* (2022). Kelly's poems have been choreographed to dance by *Voices Dance Project*, Ottawa, 2023. One of her poems has been published in the *FOLD 2023 Festival Program*, Ontario (Festival of Literary Diversity). Another one of Kelly's poems was awarded Honorable Mention - Creators of Justice Literary Awards, International Human Rights Art Festival, New York. One of her stories, published in Fragmented Voice, *Heart/h*, UK, was nominated for the Pushcart Prize 2022. Kelly was shortlisted across Canada for the *Top 25 Canadian Immigrants Awards* 2023. Her works are on the *Lunar Codex* project: her two poems and *Letters to Singapore* are going to the Moon on the *NOVA Mission One* in 2023 and on the *Griffin Mission One* in 2024

The Tree Whisperer

It is 2 p.m., the muggiest point of the day. I cannot bear the thought of trudging to the bus stop on the other side of the road in this overwhelming Singapore humidity. Every pore of my body struggles to acclimatize to my vacation. I look longingly at the taxi stand: Oh, I am second in line. Who cares what it costs, right? Guiltily, I jump into the backseat, sink back, and feel the cool air conditioner slowly revive my sanity. I barely hear the faint whisper of the driver repeating my home address as he gently veers his vehicle into the busy street. The trace of sickly sweet, perfumy fake pine from the cheap dispenser dangling over the front mirror suspends in midair. The aroma makes me homesick for Calgary.

"Excuse me. Excuse me."

I lean forward to catch the soft murmur of the taxi driver. He points to his windshield.

"Do you see any wind outside?"

I shake my head, puzzled.

The man keeps pointing, "Look in front. Look to the right. No wind, right?"

"No, no wind," I answer. I am perplexed.

The Chinese taxi driver, a small man huddled over his steering wheel, probably in his sixties, raises his voice. Now, he points out the right window of the moving car.

"Look. Look. Look at the trees. Do you see the branches moving?"

"No... no... the branches are not moving," my voice trails off in curiosity.

"Now look at the leaves at the top of the trees. See? The leaves are moving but the branches are not."

My eyes wander to the top of the giant trees that dot the road. The leaves ARE fluttering. Weird.

The taxi driver lifts his left hand from the steering wheel, and his five fingers mimic the movement of the dancing leaves.

"You see, right? No wind. No breeze. But the leaves at the top of the trees are moving."

Again, his fingers flutter. My eyes move from the trees outside on the sides of the road to his swaying fingers. I am not sure what is happening at all.

The car turns left at the traffic lights; now, the man points to the coconut and palm trees in front of some blocks of private low-rise condos. My inquisitive eyes follow his hypnotic gestures.

"Ok. Now, look at that. Can you see? Look at the long leaves of the palm trees. The movement is different. Each leaf, ah, move like this—one, two, three, four."

This time, his fingers flap up and down straightly, one at a time, like the fronds of the palm trees outside.

"I'll tell you why, ok? Even when there is no wind, the leaves are moving to get water and energy. The trees are full of energy. Can you see? Feel it. Smell it. The leaves are moving all the time and looking for water. Getting water from the ground. Getting water from the air. Large breathing trees. Human. Alive. No wind also no problem. Still alive."

At this stage, I'm spellbound. The taxi driver has my full attention. I gawk at the leaves on trees and bushes outside. I gape at the coconut trees and the palm trees as the taxi whizzes by the landscape. The line of trees never ever ends. I've never noticed them in such detail. Trees. Green. Bushes. Plants. Flowers. Buildings. Roads. That's just Singapore. The flash of concrete, machines, and nature. Always patiently there, like an unlikely juxtaposition. Yet a beautiful harmony.

Now, I can't take my eyes off nature's green moving scene. I always knew that the Singapore trees were there, all my life. This man's soft, gentle voice is soothing. I'm mesmerized: these trees and plants, their life, their movement, their energy.

"You know, if you go to other countries, you do not see so many trees. When you go to Kuala Lumpur, you feel tired because there are not too many trees around you on the streets. Then, you come back to Singapore, and you feel so much energy all around you. Look, look there now. See the leaves still moving, moving, dancing," then he chuckles. "You know what? I told this ninety-year-old Chinese man in my taxi about the dancing leaves this morning. He was so surprised. He told me he never noticed the leaves moving that much. He said he's ninety years old, and this was the first time he was hearing about them. He said from now on, he will look for the magic leaves every day."

The taxi driver's face lit up with ardent joy.

"Can you smell the trees and flowers?" I leant forward and asked. I was completely sucked in by his enthusiasm.

"Of course, lah. They smell so good. Even though the longkang, you know, the drain, or the dustbin around the blocks stinks, you just smell the trees and flowers. You know, at night, I sleep on the balcony outside under the trees. I look at the sky and stars and moon. I can hear the noisy buses and cars. I close my eyes. I smell the sweet perfume of the Singapore air. I feel like I am out in a wild forest. Not concrete jungle."

He chuckles quietly and continues, "Singapore got so many buildings. No space, lah. But the government was smart when they planted trees and bushes and flowers from a long time ago. Not cheap, you know. Each tree is over a thousand dollars. So, when you look around and see buildings, bricks, stone and concrete, you still feel like in a wonderful garden."

I nod silently, in total agreement with my fellow Singaporean who had aptly described how our government had wisely planted beautiful greenery amidst all the buildings. No cost, indeed, had been spared, and the result was an oasis of unexpected gardens.

The taxi slows down in front of my block of flats. This time, I perceive trees, trees, trees. I had never noticed them in detail before, even though I have been here for seven weeks already.

"What is your name, sir?" I ask him as I pay his fare and open the door.

"My name is Mr. Long," he smiles. "You know, every day, I tell everyone in my taxi about how the leaves and trees have life and how they move even though there is no wind. Trees are living beings. They are so powerful. Positive energy."

"Goodbye, Mr. Long," I wave at him as he slowly pulls away. The leaves on the trees around my block of flats gently sway. Pure joy. I take a slow, long deep breath and inhale the energy of Mr. Long's dancing leaves.

When I get home to my 12th floor flat, I lean over the balcony, recollecting Mr. Long—The Tree Whisperer! I ponder about being back on vacation after three quarantined years away. My home. Singapore's concrete jungle looms around me. There is a mix of government subsidized and private high-rise buildings. Shops, markets, and shopping centres dot every neighbourhood. I stare enviably at the few luxurious concrete houses, proudly encircled by brick fences—rare, expensive sanctuaries worth millions on a little island where land is rare and reclaimed. A row of tall, three-storey semi-detached houses lean into each other below. The plethora of dwellings sit in organized, unexpected fashion. Yet, every road, median, and building is carefully dotted with plants, trees, bushes—I let my eyes wander. I have forgotten about the ever-present greenery, foliage, and vegetation, having grown up here and seeing them as simply *part of Singapore*. As a young child, at school, I sat under giant trees in the school field to block the furious sun rays. I hugged trees and hid behind them when my friends and I played Hide and Seek. From my high-rise flat, I often looked down at trees. I even towered over their majestic height. At East Coast Beach, my family and I had picnics under the coconut and palm trees that swayed in the breeze from the South China Sea.

Today, Mr. Long made me realize that I had simply overlooked how Singapore was more than a giant seamless city of stones, bricks, tree trunks, bushes, flowers—continuous, smooth concrete jungle and nature knotted, fused, and intertwined. *Singapore was a true Garden City.*

The sun suffocates my senses. I wipe the rivulets of sweat with my indispensable giant white and red cowboy-patterned handkerchief. The waft of sweat upon sweat. Salty. There are so many towering blocks of flats that sit at every corner of this small island, a country crammed with 5.7 million people. Singapore, the country of my birth, is close to the size of Calgary. Singapore. Calgary. I am blessed. Truly, each country's landscape is lovingly engraved in my soul. It's all about perspectives. I am here. I am there. I am home in both Singapore and Calgary; I am an outsider, in both, at times. But in nature, in both countries, I can simply exist and be authentic.

Right now, in this spectacular moment, perched high above the canopy of trees, I soak in and celebrate the private symphony and performance the Singapore leaves have put on for me. I take a deep intense gulp of the humid air. I smile when I think of Mr. Long, The Tree Whisperer, sharing his magic gems with each and every passenger in his taxi every single day.

Marie-Denise Douyon

Le parcours de Marie-Denise Douyon, une artiste d'origine haïtienne, est marqué par le nomadisme. Elle est née à Port-au-Prince, a grandi en Afrique du Nord, étudié à New York et Washington et vit à Montréal. Elle est diplômée du Fashion Institute of Technology de New York et elle est venue au Québec en tant que réfugiée politique en 1991. L'exil a motivé cette artiste à créer pour se recréer et son art est un message d'espoir et de résilience.

L'élément déclencheur pour l'écriture de Marie-Denise a été une arrestation douloureuse en Haïti. En prison, elle a découvert que la création, l'écriture et la peinture étaient son exutoire. En 2019, elle a publié son premier ouvrage, « Mots imaginaires pour se recréer ». Pendant la pandémie en 2020, elle crée Muzikiddy ; une plateforme d'outils jeunesse innovants pour aborder les notions d'identités multiples de manière ludique auprès des enfants de 4 à 10 ans.

Ses sources d'inspiration proviennent de son amour de la langue française, des fables de Lafontaine et de proverbes. Marie-Denise puise dans un registre animalier et dans les proverbes pour nourrir son imaginaire. Elle utilise des animaux plutôt que des humains pour transmettre ses messages de manière ludique sans stigmatiser les habitants, quel que soit le lieu.

La neige n'a pas d'odeur

La neige n'a ni odeur, ni goût. Pourtant, curieusement, en ce jour apocalyptique de tempête de verglas, la neige empestait la mort. Une odeur de glace s'engouffre dans vos narines et vous gèle le cerveau. Une odeur aux relents de bave sirupeuse et d'haleine putride s'incruste sournoisement dans les fibres de mon foulard d'hiver.

Parmi un amoncellement de troncs d'arbres éventrés et de cimes de branches décapitées, entre deux pylônes électriques abattus, un enchevêtrement de câbles jonche le tapis de neige d'un parc méconnaissable. Des étincelles éparses scintillent ici et là, comme des guirlandes de Noël qui rendent l'âme sur un linceul de neige compacte. Un mince filet de fumée grisâtre s'élève en arabesque dans ce décor irréel. Des effluves de pétards mouillés de soufre traversent, furtivement, l'atmosphère.

Je continue ma promenade nocturne de photographe en quête de ce rare cliché, de cette scène inédite et exceptionnelle qui défraiera les manchettes. Autour de moi, les branches craquent et agonisent sur un grabat de glace. Chacun de mes pas fendent une calotte de givre et résonnent en un craquement de verre brisé.

Montréal, ma ville, mon refuge, s'est endormie... Sans lumière, sans chaleur et sans bruits. Le verglas a déployé son immense suaire argenté sur ma ville, mon refuge. Ensevelis sous de lourds duvets, sous d'épais manteaux de peurs et d'anxiété, les Montréalais, en état de catalepsie, sommeillent les mâchoires serrées, les jointures frigorifiées, marbrées de veines bleues.

Le verglas n'a ni odeur ni goût. Pourtant, curieusement en ce jour apocalyptique de tempête, le verglas sent la mer. De ma bouche s'échappe tel un volcan en éruption un minuscule nuage de buée imbibé de sel, d'écailles et d'algues de la Méditerranée. Un parfum salin chatouille mes narines et titille mon imagination. J'éternue ! Une explosion de postillons piégés dans mon foulard de laine assiège mon visage. J'entends le flux et reflux des vagues de mon enfance qui raisonnent en mon cœur et ma mémoire. Je vois la corniche et le bord de mer. Les chiens courent et affrontent, tels des matadors dans l'arène, l'écume des vagues. Une larme glisse et réchauffe ma joue glaciale. Je pleure de froid, de nostalgie et de regrets.

Mes jambes s'engourdissent. Un escadron de minuscules aiguilles, d'épingles et de clous de tapissier assaillent mes gros orteils. À l'abordage, le droit d'abord, ensuite le gauche. Je pense aux voyages de Gulliver et son aventure lilliputienne.

Point d'âmes vivantes à l'horizon. Le vent s'engouffre dans mon canal auditif. Il siffle, il souffle, il entonne un requiem. Un brusque et strident hurlement d'une sirène d'ambulance interrompt cet hymne lancinant. Un nuage toxique d'émanation de gaz, de carburant, d'huile à moteur s'immisce dans l'air cristallin et me prend à la gorge. Je tousse, je hoquète, je crachote. Recroquevillée, pliée en deux, je prends appui sur un tronçon d'arbre abattu. Une main invisible m'arrache les poumons.

Je m'efforce péniblement à mettre un pied devant l'autre pour avancer. Les picotements insoutenables d'aiguilles et d'épingles ont atteint mes cuisses. J'ai l'impression d'avoir mis les pieds dans une fourmilière. Chacune de mes cuisses pèse une tonne. J'aurai besoin qu'une grue me hisse, qu'un treuil me remorque. Mon esprit erre dans l'air glacial. Je pense à Neil Armstrong, le premier homme à avoir posé les pieds sur la lune. Tout comme mes jambes, mon cerveau s'engourdit. S'agissait-il de Neil ou de Louis Armstrong ? Peu importe, je ne me sens plus capable de réfléchir et de continuer à marcher. Je décide de m'arrêter, juste le temps de reprendre mon souffle. Je m'assieds sur le socle d'un tronc rasé par les vents infernaux du verglas.

L'assaut démentiel des fourmis voraces a atteint mon nombril. Des colonnes de milliers de ces bestioles grosses comme des têtes d'épingles remontent vers mes aisselles, laissant sur leur passage une trainée d'azote qui me tétanise et me gèle les membres.

Voraces et féroces comme des tarentules, elles ont tendu leur filet. Je suis prise au piège, immobilisée. Chrysalide dans un cocon de glace. Je fixe du regard les stalactites d'argent suspendues aux branches. Tout est beau, féérique, tout scintille. Je suis éblouie. Les régiments de fourmis poursuivent leurs avancées criminelles et gagnent du terrain. Elles ont franchi la ligne de mon menton et dévalent mes paupières, s'agrippent à mes cils et finissent par envahir l'iris des yeux.

Je capitule et baisse les paupières. Une lueur incandescente apparait. Les fourmis battent en retraite et mettent fin à leur terrible offensive. La trêve semble se prolonger. Je sens la brise méditerranéenne qui porte en son souffle nectars d'algues, de coquillages et de sel marin.

Je sors de mon sommeil, comme d'une courte sieste. Le parc est méconnaissable. Plus aucune trace des affres de la tempête. La neige a fondu. Du sol remonte une odeur de terre mouillée, d'humus. Les premiers crocus jaunes percent l'hymen blanc d'un mince tapis de neige humide. Un bouquet d'arômes printaniers distille l'air. Je hume à pleins poumons le parfum des fleurs et savoure le printemps, les ailes du nez écartées.

Je songe au muguet de la fête des mères et, brusquement, une odeur d'iode envahit mes souvenirs. Au loin, j'aperçois la mer et les rochers à marée basse. Les chiens courent derrière des balles, s'ébrouent vigoureusement en sortant de l'eau, les enfants construisent des châteaux de sable sur le rivage. La mer est belle mais agitée ; le bruit des vagues me berce. J'entends la voix de ma mère, celle de ma grand-mère, qui toutes deux fredonnent une berceuse en une langue inconnue. Cette langue m'enveloppe, me réconforte, me pénètre, réchauffe ma poitrine et mon cœur meurtri. Emmaillotée, je n'ai plus froid !

Je perçois deux clappements sourds et saccadés. Je tourne la tête vers la droite, une énorme cigogne vient d'atterrir à deux mètres de moi. Elle parle la langue des hommes et des dieux, elle m'invite à prendre place sur son dos. J'enfourche ses longues ailes blanches et arrondies et m'agrippe à son épais collier de plumes duveteuses. Ma joue collée à son cou, je respire sa senteur de cigogne. Étrange fragrance que celle de cet échassier. Entre cardamone et safran, entre coriandre et cumin, elle porte en ses plumes les saveurs de l'Atlas.

Elle monte à pic, au zénith et se rapproche d'une boule de feu couleur de bronze, couleur de miel. Étrange brasier, que ce brasier ovale qui réchauffe sans brûler. Cigogne et moi, nous sommes happées en plein centre de la sphère lumineuse et nous nous disséminons en des milliers de particules, d'atomes de douceur, de tendresse et de compassion. Solo, un violon pleure et gémit. Une mélodie lancinante, larmoyante envahit la voute céleste. Soudain, l'archet se met à grincer, à couiner sur les cordes des vibrations aigües, insoutenables.

Un crissement, un hurlement de sirène fend les cieux. Je suis tout à coup propulsée à l'extérieur de la sphère, ma tête explose, une douleur atroce comprime mon thorax.

Telles des lattes de volets de bambou que l'on entrebâille au matin, j'entrouvre légèrement les paupières. Autour de moi, tout est flou. Je distingue d'imperceptibles ombres et taches de lumières qui exécutent un étrange ballet. Elles semblent se mouvoir, le long d'un étroit, d'un interminable corridor. Ce spectacle m'épuise. À nouveau, je ferme les yeux.

Paupières closes, les sons sont décuplés ; grincements de roues de chariots, voix calfeutrés, bavardages incessants, claquements de portes, cet incessant bruit de fond, de sirènes qui hurlent. Pour couronner ce vacarme en ce lieu démentiel, s'entremêle un tumulte d'effluves suffocants ; odeur âcre, tenace de camphre, d'urine pestilentielle, relent de lait caillé, de beurre rance, de sang séché, de souffle nauséabond de vomissures. Je manque d'air, je pousse des râles rauques à travers un épais masque de plastique. Je respire à peine, je suffoque... À l'aide !

Je perçois un bruissement. Une voix lointaine chuchote à mon oreille de compter jusqu'à dix. De nature obéissante, je m'exécute. Un, deux, six, huit... La nuit tombe d'un coup sec, comme le couperet d'une guillotine. Qui a éteint toutes les lumières ? Une dernière pensée m'habite. Demain aux premières lueurs de l'aube, je déambulerai sur les trottoirs glacés de ma ville, – mon refuge.

Montréal... J'immortaliserai ta beauté de glace, ta splendeur d'argent. Je capterai les reflets d'acier scintillants de ton indomptable nature.

Antonio D'Alfonso

Poet, novelist, essayist, translator, Antonio D'Alfonso has published more than sixty books (including translations) and has made five feature films. Born in 1953, he is the founder of Guernica Editions which he managed for thirty-three years before passing it on to new owners in 2010. For his writings, he won the Trillium Award and the Bressani Award. His film *Bruco* won the New York Independent Film Award. He holds a Ph.D. from the University of Toronto. In 2016, he received an Honorary Doctorate from Athabasca University. His new film, *TATA (Daddy)*, was released in July 2020. *The Two-Headed Man: Collected Poems 1970-2020* was published in July 2020 (Guernica Editions). He has started on YouTube a series of *Conversations* with artists and producers. His essays of *In Italics: In Defense of Ethnicity* (1996), *Gambling With Failure* (2005), and *Poetica del plurilinguismo* (2015) offer a unique perspective on decentralized identities. His books have been translated in French, Italian, German, Spanish, Estonian, and Portuguese. He has just been published under the title, *Outside Looking In (Entries 1980-1981)* (Ekstasis Editions).

Ruskin Park

During the last months at Saint-Finbarr's Elementary, in a freshly built two-storey rectangular construction on 13th Avenue, south of Bélanger Street, boys and girls shed their winter wear and revealed slivers of skin, which for months had been covered by ten pounds of wool. We loved to exaggerate.

Emmanuel, master of mathematics, English grammar, biology, religion, you name it, Emmanuel was the best. He was ten or eleven years old. I was a friend of the school genius, and proud to be. I was not as talented. So why would Emmanuel want me as a friend? Besides both being Italian, nothing else much connected one to the other. Interestedness? I can't say.

As soon as my mother had taught me the way to school, more than two and a half miles (four kilometres) from home, every morning I would walk down 19th Avenue, cross Ruskin Street, and meet up with Emmanuel on 18th (aka Biron Avenue), where he lived.

Every morning, together we would gambol our way uphill to Bélanger Street. Chitchatting, arguing, laughing, we sauntered over the city limits—the border that separated Saint-Michel from Rosemount in Montreal—and walk through Saint-Bernadette Park.

Each and every morning, we routinely sailed into Sainte-Bernadette Church for Mass, and took Communion, before darting off to class. Yes, we were believers and often discussed Mary, Jesus, and God. I did the best I could to follow Emmanuel's reasoning, and I learned to plead my case. Emmanuel's scholarly dedication influenced me to such a degree that my grades went up for a year or two.

Emmanuel was a nervous boy. Thin, dark-skinned, he had sunken eyes and hollow cheeks, a long chin, a dark demure. He could have hopped out of a El Greco painting. He had a refined mind and conversation sat comfortably with him, even at such a young age. Prattling and debating with him filled me with such pleasure that I did not want our walks to end.

Beyond our hourly parley bubble, strangely, once in the school yard there was total silence between us. Ideas, commentaries, and opinions galore, yes, yet once in the school environment, we shared not even a glance. Our friendship, incredible to say, rested uniquely in those morning and evening walks.

I liked his intellectual intensity, and he admired my gregariousness. But Emmanuel had no sense of civility, which annoyed the hell out of me. How could such a sensitive mind have such rough edges? This inconsistency burst forth strikingly on one particular day.

It was after class and we were immersed in our philosophical argument when Emmanuel decided he wanted to kiss my friend Susan on the mouth.

Susan was not too pleased with my friend's behaviour.

I begged Emmanuel to lay off.

But he stubbornly grew more and more obsessive. He wanted Susan and nothing was going to stop him. He fell into a trance.

So odd was his conduct that I found myself grabbing him by the jacket collar. I slapped him a few times, which angered him. He punched me. I docked.

I punched him, and my fist did not miss the target. Right on the jaw.

I hurt him badly. I might have broken something.

He fell. The other kids screamed.

I tried to pull Emmanuel up to his feet; he didn't want me to touch him, didn't want me to talk to him, didn't want to walk back home together.

The following evening, my father was asked to visit the principal who scolded me for being a ruffian.

My father listened quietly to the insults directed at him, gently stood up, and calmly smiled, like only my father could when he was enraged, and spoke softly in Italian, adding a few French and English words:

"My son protected a girl's virtue. If you have a daughter, you must surely sympathize."

The principal did not sympathize. He gave me the strap, six times on each hand.

Like Emmanuel the day before, I did not weep, regardless of the pain.

What made me turn on my friend?

Was I reacting out of jealousy?

Perhaps I had a crush on Susan but, at eleven, I was too young to entertain such amorous feelings. Ours was more an affinity for clothes, fragrances, attitude, something I didn't find with the guys.

Susan, a Romanian, was like an Italian. That ethnic bond must have tickled my curiosity.

Was my father's comment justified? Was I brought up to defend my younger sister?

I believed that Susan, being my sister's friend, needed my help, as though it were incumbent on me to intervene and defend her honour.

I asked myself if boys without sisters behaved differently from boys with sisters? This would have been a great topic for one of our morning discussions. What would have been his take on the issue?

Emmanuel had no sister. He who was such an elegant mind was a bully in the flesh. He demonstrated a vulgarity I hadn't noticed until that precise moment. Ideas, it seemed, belonged to a sphere of activity that had nothing to do with the quotidian gestures of boy-girl graciousness and understanding.

That unfortunate incident put an end to our relationship. Hurting a buddy physically was a turning point for me. Emmanuel's pride had been bruised, and there was no excuse that was going to erase the blemish.

I looked at Emmanuel, and he looked at me. Why couldn't we make amends when the pain subsided? We didn't.

The emotional leap—the jump over the pile of delusions—would become, in the future, the barometer of friendship. Quarrel all you will, for years if must be, but when the time comes, let's roll up our sleeves and get back to friend-shipping.

Being physical was out of the ordinary for me. I never was, and still am not, a tough person. Rather shy as a boy, with a loud laugh, I was the funny one compared to the tough guys in our class.

I avoided fights, and I played no sports. Whenever I did, be it hockey, baseball, or football, I would irremediably crash.

I got in the habit of breaking a piece of me.

I was more into clothes, shoes, and music. I enjoyed studying boys and girls playing their seduction games in the schoolyard and in the park. My mind wandered elsewhere. I paid special attention to my female teachers. Even in third grade, I preferred mature women. I got the strap for gazing at Mrs. Keyes's thighs once.

Pretty much on my own, hair growing long, with bangs covering my forehead, and overdressed for all occasions, I could be irascible, as I became once over my expensive school briefcase. I was particularly embarrassed by the vintage saddle school briefcase with its military pattern that my parents had purchased. Even if practical, such flamboyancy simply didn't suit me. The militia look didn't become me. I tried to explain myself, but my parents refused to listen.

Nevertheless, the Teddy Boy persona was for older boys, not me. Elvis Presley and Ricky Nelson were before my time.

I adopted a modish style which would, a decade later, be called the boogaloo look. That was 1962 or 1963, a few years before Flower Power hippied its way into our lives. I found the sober Beatles' attire more to my liking. I was certainly not going to slip on a black leather jacket and grease my hair back.

While other boys were busy skating or learning to fix cars, I chose to take private music lessons for the guitar. I loved to dance to the riff of "Shaking All Over" by Johnny Chester with the Thunderbirds. I still own the 45 rpm of the record.

Of course, if I was asked, I accepted to be part of the team and stood in front of the net. My career as a goalie, though, ended rather quickly and embarrassingly: the puck made its way not to the end of the net, but right on my lips.

Sports were not my forte.

Imagine, I ended my school year at Saint-Finbarr's with a bandage wrapped around my head. That undoctored wound had surely hidden a concussion. Yet I refused to go to the hospital and never received stitches. My parents trusted my decision. Decades later, however, that spot on my head is still sensitive. It's psychosomatic more than any real pain.

All that is to say that I preferred the presence of girls to that of boys, conversations with girls in the park to volleyball or football competitions.

One good example of my misadventures in the parks with the boys happened on Ruskin Street, between Biron (18th Avenue) and Dante (Leonard da Vinci), where the city administration built, as an afterthought, a playground for children and a rectangular space reserved for bocce for the Italian men in the neighbourhood. There was a swing or two and a brick cabin where toys were stored in the evening. During the day, the cabin served as a workshop for crafts.

In the summer, children were expected to register in order to participate in the park activities. Not very respectful of authority, I did not bother to register. I contented myself with meeting other kids later in the evening, once the person in charge carried in the toys and locked the doors to the cabin.

After supper, we returned to the playground and indulged in a game of baseball or sat and bantered on the swing until sunset.

Then, one day, the park was empty. No one was there. I noticed the cabin doors were open and stepped inside. A workshop on unfolding. Some of the kids from the neighbourhood were there, hands covered with clay.

I sat on a bench and listened to the young woman explaining the rudiments of clay-making. Speaking French, the assistant handed me a ball of clay and invited me to patiently follow her instructions. And so, little by little, I fashioned the ball into some sort of dish. I was surprised, ecstatic, by this creative feat.

Revelling in the joy of what can be achieved with a ball of clay, I decided to stay in the class, and stared as a young man parked his bike outside. He bounced in and said hello to his assistant. He counted the number of kids present, one, two, three, up to ten.

He looked at a pad and pronounced the names of the boys and girls present. Once finished, he turned to me: "You're not on my list."

I whispered my name, staring at his running shoes.

He promptly ordered me out.

"Why?" I asked in English.

The monitor turned to his more empathetic assistant and said in French: "He doesn't belong here."

"The park is for everyone," I retorted, before the assistant could open her mouth.

"Yes, the park is for everyone," the watchdog interrupted. "Workshops are for boys and girls who have registered for this pottery class."

"I had no idea I had to register."

"That's the rule."

"Change the rule," I said casually, arrogantly.

"Your manners?" The monitor pointed to the door. "Get out of the cabin."

"I'm staying," I insisted.

The young man grabbed me with his two hands and threw me out of the cabin.

I have no idea where I got the energy or will power, but my fists hit him on his cheeks, my kicks against his chest. He, in his early twenties; I, eleven twelve.

The monitor threw me out of the park and onto the sidewalk. "You're banned from this park for the rest of the summer."

That was it for me: never again was I able to visit Ruskin Park during the day. When it was time for summer festivities and four of us offered to perform on the Roulotte stage, miming a few songs by The Beatles, our show had to be given in another park: Saint-Damase Park on Dickens Street and 20th Avenue.

Saint-Bernadette's Park, Ruskin Park, and Saint-Damase Park: the three parks that appear in my childhood.

What happened to Susan, Emmanuel?

Susan married Carlo, a friend, I still frequent today.

Emmanuel? Rumour has it that he had gone crazy after high school and that his mother had found her son hanging in the basement of their home on 18th Avenue, a few metres south of Ruskin Park.

Me? I learned to play guitar and, in the evenings, when there was no monitor, I sometimes played baseball as a catcher, until the inevitable occurred.

The boy at the base plate vigorously struck the ball out of Ruskin Park limits. His skinny body uncontrollably followed the swinging bat, which gleefully did a full 360-degree circle before whacking me right on the back of my head.

A horrified Mrs. Peccia, a neighbour, who walked onto the balcony to shake off the bread crumbs from the table cloth, must have noticed the blood pouring out of the wound, and immediately ran into the park with bandage and hydrogen peroxide. She wrapped a towel around my head, and caringly led me back to the safety of our home. With all the buzzing in my head, what I remember is the reassuring fragrance of rapini, roasted garlic, and olive oil on her dark skin.

Barbara D. Janusz

The author of the Calgary Herald best-selling novel, *Mirrored in the Caves*, Barbara D. Janusz has also published short stories, poetry, book reviews, editorials, and creative non-fiction in literary journals, magazines, newspapers, and anthologies across Canada. She is a mother, lawyer, environmentalist, feminist, and educator. A graduate of the University of Alberta, in Edmonton where she was born and raised, Barbara has also resided on Canada's West Coast, in Crowsnest Pass, La Paz, Mexico and Paris, France. A longstanding member of the Writers Guild of Alberta, Barbara has been a contributing writer for *EnviroLine*, *Alternatives Journal*, *Wild Lands Advocate*, *Herizons*, and *ARTiculate Magazines*. She currently makes her home in Calgary.

Hammerheads at Balandra Bay

The black volcanic cordillera loomed like a wavy mirage, and yet its mirror image in the shallow cove barely triggered a ripple. At low tide, it was possible to wade across to the other side without getting wet above the waist. The water would have felt like a bath with the temperature hovering in the mid-forties, that late August afternoon. But we abstained from spending the afternoon in the shallow, outlying cove of Balandra Bay and decided, instead, to savour the coolness of the sea breeze wafting beyond the labyrinth of volcanic rock caves that ushered in the open sea.

I was also anxious to discover whether Balandra's famous landmark—the balanced rock, ensconced on a point of lava ledges—was still intact. An igneous monolith, supported by a pivot of lava, the balanced rock was molded eons ago from magma spewing out of a crater and then abruptly cooling. In 1996, the rock attracted the wrath of vandals. Its destruction elicited such widespread condemnation, that the expatriates of La Paz appealed to the scientific community for a viable method to salvage Balandra's geologic treasure. An American chemist, (a woman, no less), took up the challenge and concocted a glue with the requisite Herculean grip to bond the spherical chunk of lava rock to its pillared stone base.

Lowering my head to pass through one of the more protuberant rock overhangs of volcanic caverns, I sensed my nostrils crinkle in response to the pungent, salty air. A sticky smell, the sea breeze conjured images of pelicans taking flight upon the sun's angled descent toward the horizon. At least we didn't have to watch where we stepped. The erosive force of the sea's ebb and flow that, at high tide, churned within the molded recesses of the grotto had, over eons, scoured the volcanic bedrock. At ebb tide, it was like walking upon an even slate floor.

We emerged from the caverns, onto the stretch of strand that curved toward the volcanic shelf upon which the balanced rock kept watch like a sentinel. The surf supplanted the silence. A gust of wind—like a silk scarf—caressed our faces and drew my eyes toward the half dozen sailboats anchored in Balandra Bay. For centuries, the bay, a hurricane hold, had sheltered navigators of the Sea of Cortez from the ravages of annual tropical storms. It was within its confines that my five-year-old son, Olek, and I stumbled upon the ecological disaster.

From a distance, it appeared as a grey mound of refuse, with innumerable flies swarming overhead. As we drew closer, we caught wind of the horrible stench—unmistakably a reek of rotting marine flesh. Perhaps we should have turned back, towards the tranquil confines of the cover, but I had a sinister impulse to discover what lay ahead.

The stench and flies didn't permit us to get too close. While Olek instinctively covered his nose with his hand, I was forced to take in shallow breaths. At first what was staring me in the face didn't register. Like an optical illusion, the hundreds of discarded decapitated hammerheads, piled on top of one another, appeared to form some grotesque configuration. It finally hit me that a fishing boat, laden with an enormous catch of hammerhead sharks, had dumped the wastage onto shore. I visualized the hunters, armed with machetes, decapitating one shark after another, their bodies emitting their final tremors as their hammer-shaped heads were savagely severed from their bodies.

Firmly taking my son by the hand, I shot a glance backwards towards the balanced rock—its dark profile silhouetted against the undulated aquamarine waves of the open sea. I wanted to forget the discarded hammerheads, but instead, as we retraced our footprints in the sand, I reasoned the fishermen likely harbored the misconception that hammerhead sharks are in endless supply.

Unlike other sharks, hammerheads form schools that attract hundreds of individuals. Believed by marine biologists to reduce the risk of predation from larger sharks, the schools, unfortunately, render hammerheads easy prey from commercial fishing vessels. Bent on satisfying the growing and insatiable international demand for shark meat and fins, the vessel that dumped the hammerhead craniums on the beach obviously didn't have any appreciation for conservation and, like today's transnational corporations, was maximizing its potential to earn a profit.

Sharks are ancient creatures, at the top of the marine food chain. Over the past decades, shark populations worldwide have been steadily declining. In the case of hammerheads, this trend is particularly alarming as they possess a peculiar habit of scavenging along ocean beds. Sometimes referred to as "swimming noses," hammerheads swim in a zigzag pattern, swinging their heads from side to side—as if they were operating a metal detector—tracking the scent of wounded or diseased prey. Their extraordinarily positioned noses have evolved amazing sensors, called *ampullae Lorenzini*, that allow them to detect weak electrical fields and chemical and thermal changes in the water, even the heartbeat of injured prey.

Early Hawaiians revered and did not commonly catch or eat hammerheads. The sharks' scavenging habits were recognized as vital for preserving their marine habitat. Geologically, the Hawaiian Islands, like Balandra Bay, were formed by volcanic eruptions. The hypersensitive sensory characteristic of the hammerhead's nose also facilitates the detection of magnetic fields, generated by seismic activity. A hammerhead lured far from its school, while tracking injured prey, is innately equipped to find its way back to familiar waters.

As we trekked back up the narrow expanse of beach towards the cove, I realized that Olek, all the while, had remained uncharacteristically quiet. He didn't inquire about what we'd just witnessed on the beach, nor why it smelled so putridly.

A slim band of shadows now extended from the western flank of volcanic ridge that ringed the cove onto the beach. It didn't feel much cooler in the shade on account of the still air, but I needed to collect my thoughts before getting behind the wheel of my truck to drive the twenty-two kilometre stretch of asphalt back to La Paz. Although I'd been to Balandra many times, until then, I'd never found an analogy between its lava ridges and the decaying walls of a Roman amphitheater. The surrounding volcanic rock exuded a metallic odour—like rusted iron—similar to that of ancient ruins. Looking down onto the aquamarine waters of the cove, I felt as though I was perched in the cavea—the seating area of the coliseum.

I drank in the scenic tranquility of the cove—a colony of frigates suspended in an updraft of sea air—and inhaled. The dry desert air stubbornly countered the persistence of odours. In the heat of the day, the odourless air of the desert reminded me of clothes coming out of a dryer, but after a deluge, during hurricane season, the Saguaro cacti forests that thrived below the summits of the Baja California volcanic cordillera, emitted green vegetal scents, redolent of moisture laden mosses in woodlands, with their distinctive woodsy-earthy perfume. After a good rain, flowers sprouted from the parched vines that radiated across the terracotta hued earth, but these flora didn't emit any perceptible scent. Desert flowers, it seemed, whenever sufficient moisture permitted, conserved all their energy to blossom.

When I breathed in again, to my dismay, the malodorous scent of the rotting marine flesh still lingered in my nostrils. It reminded me of the tenacious foul spray unleased by skunks as a defense mechanism that burns in the recesses of the nose, and I couldn't banish the surreal image of the grey mound of marine flesh with the hordes of flies buzzing overhead.

I thought of the ancient Hawaiians and their reverence for hammerheads. Maybe laws that prohibit poaching, laying waste, and polluting need to be rooted in reverence for other life forms. In order to embrace a belief system that is entrenched in conservation and humility, it may be incumbent upon us to edit history, to shift the focus of our narrative from the arrogant prowess and conquests of monarchs and pharaohs to mythologizing the more benign saga of our relationship with the ecosystems that sustained us for tens of thousands of years.

Our evolution wasn't triggered by our domestication of wild grains and animals, the cultivation of crops and the dawning of the agrarian age. It was preceded by a much longer era in which we honed our survival instincts as hunter-gatherers, our animal instincts and our five senses of sight, hearing, touch, taste, and smell. The Neolithic civilizations that we've eulogized for their cultural achievements were indebted to their hunter-gatherer ancestors whose survival was intertwined with nature and the knowledge that they painstakingly acquired about the natural world.

But not all primeval belief systems are founded on reverence for nature. A belief system that went terribly wrong is epitomized by the crumbling, eerie-looking moai, or carved volcanic stone monoliths that stand guard over the denuded, despoiled landscape of Easter Island. The natives of this south Pacific tropical paradise cut down every last tree on the island so that they could move and erect these strange looking icons, some of which tower ten metres and weigh over fourteen tons. Instead of venerating the moai, the natives of Easter Island would have been better served by revering the trees that furnished habitat for native land and seabirds and conserved the soil that they'd traditionally cultivated for crops. Anthropologists, who've grappled with the enigma of how and why the Easter Islanders carved the gigantic moai, can only speculate about what motivated this civilization to persist in their destructive behaviour to the point of self-annihilation. It might have been a simple matter of one-upmanship—the islanders competing with one another, endeavouring to build bigger and more massive moai, and to erect them in increasingly more imposing locations.

A flock of sandpipers scurrying along the shoreline distracted me from my ruminations about man's origins and I began to wonder why we were the only ones, that afternoon, seeking a little reprieve from the stifling heat of the city. As an expatriate, I often felt as though I was out of the loop. In this heat, it wouldn't have taken long before the mound of hammerhead flesh began to reek. Perhaps yesterday, a party of beachcombers had chanced upon the mound of hammerheads and word of the slaughter had escaped my radar. Sitting on the beach, self-absorbed in shock, I was like the paralyzed bystander of a robbery or brutal assault. But what could I do? I didn't have a camera with me, and even if I did, to whom would I send the photo? In the face of ecological degradation, media sensationalism has numbed most of us into doing little more than shake our heads in dismay.

The two metal barrels ensconced in the parking lot, overlooking the cove that served as refuse containers, overflowed with all kinds of smelly garbage. The rubbish had a rotten egg, soured milk smell. As I skirted the mangrove swamp and headed south, back to La Paz, through the desert canyon, I zeroed in on all the trash—plastic bags, disposable diapers, beer and soda pop cans—that littered the desert landscape. After picnicking at the beach, few people bothered to lug their garbage back with them to the city. I observed turkey vultures—with their blood-red heads and ragged, expansive wingspans—hovering over the jagged volcanic peaks. With their keen sense of smell—like hammerheads—buzzards hone in on a decomposing carcass. They steer clear, though, of all the rubbish strewn along the highway.

Eventually, the periodic rise and fall of the ocean currents would wash the hammerhead craniums back out to sea, but I knew that, unlike the frenzied pace of modern human civilization, nature takes its time to balance itself out. The pile of hammerheads was so huge, it could take months, even years, before evidence of the slaughter stopped rolling in with the tide.

From then on, whenever I'd think about Balandra Bay, I'd be reminded of the hammerheads. The stench of rotting marine flesh had lodged itself inside my nostrils. I could still smell it and I felt dismay over another person's greedy careless disregard for our beautiful planet having altered my perception of a place that I venerated, held very dearly to my heart. It was like the vandals who'd kicked the hell out of the balanced rock. Every time I ventured up the beach to revisit the geological wonder, I felt anxious about whether the American chemist's glue was still doing its trick, or whether another group of hooligans had unleased its wrath upon this amazing natural wonder.

Veering around a curve and out of the canyon, downwards towards the Port of Pichilingue, my thoughts careened towards the ancient Greek myth of Sisyphus. Condemned to an endless struggle of rolling an enormous stone up a mountain, Sisyphus, obstinately—even when the rock, so close to the summit, incessantly rolled back down to the bottom—persisted in discharging his burden. Sisyphus, I came to realize, symbolized defiance of despair. Chained, destined to relentlessly withstand the struggle, he had no choice but to take pride in having been "chosen" to toil at such an impossible task. In the same vein as the balancing rock defied gravity, it was incumbent upon me, and others likeminded, to overcome feelings of powerlessness, demoralization, despair and, like the primordial Hawaiians, to embrace—even in the face of wholesale degradation—reverence as a credo for planet Earth and all its precious life forms.

Diego Creimer

Communicateur et militant écologiste de longue date, Diego Creimer a occupé au cours des onze dernières années différents postes à la Société pour la nature et les parcs du Canada, la Fondation David Suzuki et Greenpeace Canada, tant en communication qu'en gestion. Avant de rejoindre le mouvement environnemental, il a travaillé comme journaliste pour CBC / Radio-Canada International. En 2018, il a co-écrit un recueil d'essais sur la transition écologique, *Demain le Québec*, publié par les éditions La Presse. Il a aussi participé à plusieurs recueils de nouvelles depuis les années 1990, et co-fondé la revue de littérature hispano-canadienne *The Apostles Review*, publiée de 2005 à 2021. Originaire de la ville de La Plata en Argentine, il vit à Montréal depuis plus de 20 ans.

Le baobab de Verdun

Au milieu du bassin Sainte-Catherine — ce grand élargissement du fleuve Saint-Laurent entre les rapides de Lachine et le pont Champlain — se tient une petite île minuscule et courageuse, un rocher têtu couvert d'arbustes qui s'élève à peine à la surface de l'eau comme un grain de beauté vert. C'est l'île Rock, que certaines cartes mentionnent, mais que seuls les ornithologues et les kayakistes du coin peuvent nommer. Sur cette île qui fait face aux berges de Verdun, à la grande île aux hérons et à la pointe est de la presqu'île du parc des rapides, a poussé au milieu des années deux mille un baobab.

La graine de ce premier et, à ce jour, unique spécimen de baobab québécois à avoir poussé en nature est arrivée à Montréal un jour d'avril, vers la fin des années 1990, dans la valise d'un réfugié sénégalais du peuple soninké appelé Abdourahmane Khouma. Tenant la main d'Abdourahmane dans l'aéroport de Mirabel se trouvait sa fille Aïssé. Pendant que les agents d'Immigration Canada vérifiaient leurs papiers, Aïssé découvrait avec appréhension l'odeur chimique de la moquette et des bureaux en formica, si différente des parfums de gingembre séché et de poivre noir du marché aux épices de Diawara où elle avait flâné avec son frère Babacar dans son enfance.

Ce même jour, dans une salle de cours de l'école secondaire Mariano Moreno de la ville de Paraná, en Argentine, Leopoldo Castro prenait des notes dans son cours de biologie végétale de cinquième année. On y expliquait la reproduction des plantes et comment, au-delà des pollinisateurs plus connus comme les abeilles et les oiseaux, certains mammifères permettent aussi la reproduction d'espèces emblématiques quand ils mangent et transportent dans leurs ventres, parfois sur de longues distances, les graines contenues dans les fruits. La professeure donnait alors l'exemple des fleurs des baobabs africains qui émettent un parfum puissant dont les chauves-souris raffolent. Grisée par le nectar des fleurs, pèlerinant d'un arbre à l'autre, cette gent trotte-menu ailée assure une pollinisation croisée efficace. À un tel point que l'on retrouve des baobabs sur presque tout le continent africain.

Vingt ans plus tard, Leopoldo donnerait ce même exemple aux étudiants de son cours de biologie au Collège de Rosemont, à Montréal. Mais il expliquerait aussi la reproduction des plantes à son fils Émile, lors de leurs longues promenades en poussette, et ensuite à vélo, sur les berges de Verdun, quartier qu'il a toujours habité depuis son arrivée à Montréal, et dont la végétation du littoral du fleuve, mélange hétéroclite d'herbiers, joncheraies et arbres exotiques à moitié plantés sur d'anciens dépotoirs, s'accorde infailliblement avec sa fascination pour le monde végétal.

– Papa, pourquoi les saules pleureurs ont l'air tristes ? lui demanda le petit Émile l'été de ses cinq ans, lors d'une marche jusqu'au refuge des oiseaux migrateurs à ville Lasalle, juste à l'ouest de Verdun.

Leopoldo eut envie de lui donner une explication scientifique, lui parler de l'évolution des espèces, lui expliquer que le nom ne voulait rien dire sur l'arbre. Mais la réponse qui sortit de sa bouche fut tout autre :

– Parce que les enfants ne veulent pas monter sur eux.

Cette réponse qui se voulut une blague entraîna des conséquences immédiates. Leopoldo et son épouse Gabrielle passèrent le reste de l'été à aider Émile à monter sur les branches des saules pleureurs perchés sur le fleuve.

*

Le matin du 9 avril 1989, assis sur les rives d'un autre fleuve bien loin de Verdun, Babacar et sa sœur Aïssé lançaient des pierres dans l'eau stagnante. C'était un dimanche pas comme les autres dans la ville de Diawara. La journée s'annonçait torride et les gens étaient nerveux. Leur mère Coumba avait installé l'étal aux épices sur la rue principale, pendant qu'Abdourahmane fixait une nouvelle antenne de télévision sur le toit de leur maison, en bordure du village. La rumeur voulait que des bergers peuls mauritaniens eussent traversé le fleuve Sénégal, asséché depuis des mois par l'absence des pluies, et que leurs troupeaux de bœufs s'étaient approchés des champs de maïs dont la récolte s'annonçait déjà maigre.

Soudain, entre deux cailloux lancés à la surface endormie de l'eau, sous le ciel bleu immaculé, des coups de feu retentirent au loin. Le village au complet put les entendre, et ce ne fut qu'une question de minutes avant que le bouche-à-oreille ne fasse le tour des rues et des maisons : des bergers mauritaniens auraient tué deux hommes près du village. Sans le comprendre encore, Babacar et Aïssé étaient témoins du début de la guerre entre le Sénégal et la Mauritanie.

*

Le matin du 11 octobre 2019, Leopoldo sortit en pyjama sur le perron de sa maison de la rue Ethel à Verdun. C'était une journée froide d'automne. Le vent de l'ouest amenait des relents du fumier des champs de la Montérégie. Gabrielle sortit derrière lui, tenant le petit Émile par la main, prenant une grande respiration résignée sous le poids écrasant du sac à dos du petit qu'elle transportait toujours lors de cette petite marche rituelle de trois coins de rue qui séparait leur maison de l'école Notre-Dame-des-Sept-Douleurs. Leopoldo embrassa Gabrielle. Il sentit dans ses lèvres encore engourdies la tiédeur de la nuit qui avait collé à son corps.

Il se pencha vers Émile, l'embrassa sur la tête. Les cheveux ébouriffés de son fils sentaient encore la mousse du bain à la lavande.

Sur d'autres perrons, escaliers, pas de porte, jardins et balcons, d'autres papas et d'autres mamans embrassaient leurs enfants qui partaient à l'école. C'était le début d'une journée de va-et-vient ordinaire.

Leopoldo regarda quelques instants Gabrielle et Émile s'éloigner sur le trottoir. Puis il se tourna pour rentrer chez lui. À ce moment exact, Abdourahmane et Aïssé sortaient de l'appartement au rez-de-chaussée du duplex juste à côté, l'un poussant le bac des poubelles, l'autre tirant le petit bac de compost.

Abdourahmane était un homme grand qui semblait toujours regarder plus loin que les autres. C'est qu'il était à moitié aveugle. L'onchocercose, que les gens en Afrique et en Amérique latine appellent simplement « cécité des rivières », avait avancé d'une manière irréversible avant qu'il ne puisse avoir accès à des traitements efficaces pour l'arrêter. Il était difficile de juger ce qu'il pouvait ou ne pouvait pas voir exactement, s'il s'agissait de contours flous ou des contrastes de lumière assez nets pour assurer ses repères, mais sa condition ne l'avait pas empêché de trouver un travail dans un centre communautaire de la Pointe-Saint-Charles où il aidait dans la confection des boîtes d'une banque alimentaire. Il n'était pas capable de lire les étiquettes des produits, mais un sens surdéveloppé de l'espace et du toucher compensait ce manque. Ses collègues prenaient soin de bien distribuer les produits dans l'espace autour de lui, et ensuite Abdourahmane assemblait les boîtes comme un robot bien programmé. Les couleurs, les ombres et les formes le guidaient sans faille. Dans un monde destiné à l'obscurité, Abdourahmane s'en était construit un autre de lumière.

Les poubelles déposées soigneusement sur le trottoir, Abdourahmane rebroussait les vingt pas qui le séparaient de sa maison et levait son bras pour dire bonjour à Leopoldo quand un crissement de pneus, un freinage long et violent déchira le matin. Le reste fut un mélange de cris, pleurs et sirènes d'ambulance.

Sous le pied implacable d'un chauffard, la vie de Leopoldo venait de chambouler à jamais.

*

Il y avait beaucoup de monde aux funérailles d'Émile et de Gabrielle. Sa famille à elle, ses amis, les collègues de Leopoldo, des parents des copains d'école d'Émile, la mairesse de Verdun et le chef de police du poste de quartier 16. Une foule triste et uniforme, la nuit blanche accrochée encore aux paupières.

Abdourahmane et Aïssé y restèrent plus longtemps que les autres. Les lèvres du vieil homme, assis dans un coin du salon, murmuraient une sourate. Aïssé lui tenait la main. Leopoldo eut la force de remercier tout le monde pour leurs mots doux et solidaires. Mais il voulut néanmoins aller seul répandre les cendres sous le saule pleureur au bord des rapides.

*

Les arbres disaient adieu aux dernières feuilles. Le soleil timide du début novembre allongeait les ombres des passants. Leopoldo marcha le long des berges, vers l'ouest. Des cris d'autres enfants se faufilaient entre les branches dénudées, des voix rieuses mélangées aux grincements des manèges. Dans un coude du sentier, Leopoldo s'arrêta pour regarder une petite fille assise sur la première branche d'un tilleul. Ses parents étaient au pied de l'arbre. Toute l'étendue de sa perte rentrait dans les petits souliers blancs de la fille, se balançant par-dessus la tête de sa mère.

Leopoldo les quitta du regard. Il ajusta les bretelles de son sac à dos et poursuivit son chemin. « De moins en moins d'enfants grimpent aux arbres de nos jours, » pensa-t-il vaguement, « Aujourd'hui, les arbres s'ennuient des enfants. »

*

Il était reclus dans un silence intérieur quand la poudre grise et blanche toucha les racines du saule pleureur et la surface ondulée des eaux. La voix grave d'Abdourahmane le ramena au monde autour de lui.

— Je viens souvent ici, là où je peux marcher sans aide. Ma canne blanche et le bord de la piste cyclable s'entendent à merveille. J'y viens regarder cette petite île en face de nous, qui pour moi n'est qu'un point diffus, parfois vert, parfois noir.

— Qu'est-ce qu'il y a dans ce rocher qui vous fascine autant ?

— Un baobab.

— C'est impossible, répondit Leopoldo. Un baobab ne pourrait jamais pousser au Québec en pleine nature.

— Si, je vous le dis. C'est moi qui l'ai planté.

— C'est une espèce des régions tropicales sèches. Il ne pourrait jamais avoir poussé ici.

Leopoldo était gêné dans son rituel solitaire. Sous les yeux voilés du vieil homme, les mains de Leopoldo tenaient encore le petit coffre d'où il venait de répandre les cendres de sa famille.

— Tu viendras voir avec moi. Ça pourrait t'aider.

*

Aïssé et Babacar coururent rejoindre leur mère. La journée, jusque-là si paisible et banale, prenait un tournant tragique. Les gens se précipitaient dans toutes les directions sur la rue principale, la poussière s'élevant de la terre battue. Les enfants trouvèrent l'étal de leur mère par terre, quelques bocaux et sacs d'épices abandonnés. Ils continuèrent alors leur course affolée vers la maison, à la limite est du village, près du cimetière.

Soudain, la rage monte dans l'air chaud du matin. Les rares fenêtres et portes ouvertes se ferment avec fracas. On entend des cris de protestation à l'ouest, et le vrombissement des moteurs vers l'est. Aïssé et Babacar se trouvent coincés entre les paysans soninkés et un peloton de l'armée mauritanienne qui a traversé le fleuve asséché du côté de Yelingara.

La confusion est maintenant totale. Les paysans lancent des pierres en direction de l'armée, qui répond avec des tirs en l'air, d'abord. Mais les fronts se rapprochent. L'accrochage est inévitable. Aïssé et Babacar se collent au mur d'une maison quand l'armée tire en l'air d'abord, et sur la foule en colère ensuite.

C'est la débandade. Les tirs se poursuivent. Les soldats visent les pieds des villageois. Une balle touche Babacar au mollet gauche. L'enfant crie et s'affaisse dans les bras de Aïssé. Il commence à saigner profusément. Aïssé le traîne avec elle dans une petite rue transversale. L'armée mauritanienne avance sans les repérer. Ils s'éloignent encore jusqu'à la limite des maisons.

Aïssé et Babacar avancent péniblement par le flanc sud du village. Ils regagnent leur maison quelques minutes plus tard, essoufflés et en panique. L'antenne de télévision s'est écroulée sur un muret mitoyen, les tiges métalliques tordues au hasard, témoins silencieux de ce moment qui a changé à jamais la vie d'une famille soninké. La porte est ouverte. Il n'y a personne à l'intérieur.

Babacar continue de saigner. Avec une grande guenille en coton, Aïssé improvise un tourniquet. Il faut que leurs parents reviennent. Babacar ne tiendra pas longtemps.

*

Comme tant d'enfants de la province argentine d'Entre Ríos, Leopoldo avait grandi sur l'eau. Le balancement d'une chaloupe était pour lui aussi naturel que la fermeté d'un trottoir. L'odeur de la vase remuée par l'hélice du petit quinze chevaux lui était aussi connue, cette pourriture intemporelle d'où nénuphars et herbiers poussent vers la surface, bercés par les courants.

Abdourahmane aida Leopoldo à monter sur la proue de la chaloupe en aluminium, au quai de Verdun.

— Est-ce que tu as un permis de bateau ? lui demanda Leopoldo, inquiet.

— Non, et toi ? répliqua Abdourahmane. Je sais que tu penses à mes yeux. Je vois encore assez bien les contours et les contrastes, et je connais ce fleuve comme j'ai connu dans une autre vie le fleuve Sénégal depuis les rives de mon village. Tiens, si tu veux, je te laisserai conduire. Je peux te guider. La traversée jusqu'à l'île Rock ne dure que quelques minutes.

Leopoldo accepta de bon gré. Somme toute, il se sentait plus en sécurité aux commandes de la petite embarcation.

— Largue les amarres, ordonna Abdourahmane, et viens prendre la barre.

La chaloupe recula un peu avant de s'élancer dans une grande accélération vers l'ouest, à contre-courant. Le vacarme du moteur souleva au passage une volée de canards qui flottaient nonchalants sur l'eau verte.

Quelques minutes plus tard, les deux amis lançaient le grappin sur les galettes de la minuscule île Rock. Un vent vous décoiffait hommes et plantes. Au fond, vers l'est, les gratte-ciels de Montréal sciaient l'horizon. Abdourahmane avança d'un pas sûr, guidé par une carte imaginaire que lui seul pouvait voir. Il traîna Leopoldo au centre du rocher et s'agenouilla devant un arbre très étrange et en même temps très familier.

— Un baobab peut pousser au Québec. Voici la preuve, dit le vieil aveugle.

Leopoldo n'en croyait pas ses yeux. Lui, qui voyait si bien, assistait au miracle de celui qui ne voyait presque rien. Ses mains se mirent à caresser le tronc frêle. Le baobab devait avoir une quinzaine d'années, et il poussait en force, comme sous le soleil de l'Afrique.

— Tu te demandes comment est-ce possible. Je me suis demandé la même chose, mille fois. Ton esprit scientifique essaie de nier ce que tes mains et tes yeux lui rendent en ce moment. Je ne te juge pas. Ceci relève d'un miracle que, moi non plus, je n'arrive pas à m'expliquer. Mais laisse-moi te raconter mon histoire encore une fois, et tu comprendras peut-être ; si ce n'est par la voie de la raison, au moins par celle de l'absurde.

Il prit une grande respiration, posa ses mains sur son visage, comme pour soutenir le poids de ses souvenirs, et poursuivit :

Quand la guerre des bergers éclata dans mon pays en 1989, mon village, Diawara, a été l'épicentre des premières violences. J'ai perdu là-bas ma femme Coumba et mon fils Babacar dans les affrontements avec l'armée mauritanienne. Coumba a été piétinée par notre propre foule en pleine débandade. Pendant que j'essayais de lui prêter secours, Babacar, qui avait reçu une balle dans la jambe, saignait jusqu'au dernier souffle dans les bras de Aïssé. Comme toi, dans l'espace d'un matin lumineux, j'ai perdu presque toute ma famille.

La culpabilité de ne pas avoir été au bon endroit au bon moment pour les aider m'écrasait. Même si les violences ont assez vite cessé à Diawara pour se transporter ailleurs au pays, j'ai décidé de ramasser tout ce qui nous restait, meubles, épices et étals, et de partir avec Aïssé nous réfugier à Fadial, dans l'ouest du pays, où je connaissais Ibrahima, l'intendant du souk, à qui j'avais déjà passé des commandes. Moyennant une commission, il pourrait convaincre les autres commerçants de nous laisser nous installer en périphérie du marché. C'est là, près de Fadial, que se trouve le plus grand et le plus vieux baobab de l'Afrique, qu'on appelle avec révérence « le baobab sacré ». J'y reviendrai.

Sans surprise, et à un prix élevé, mon idée a fonctionné, mais l'emplacement de notre étal n'était pas bon et on ne vendait presque rien. On louait une chambre dans une maison de famille près du souk. Aïssé m'aidait beaucoup au travail, mais la vérité était qu'il n'y avait pas grand-chose à faire. Notre marchandise s'écoulait au compte-gouttes. J'ai décidé de vendre presque tous les meubles qui nous restaient pour qu'Aïssé puisse finir ses études secondaires. Ce fut probablement l'une de seules bonnes idées que j'ai eues dans ces années-là.

En 1991 nous avons fait connaissance de Benoît, un ingénieur forestier sénégalais de Casamance qui vivait à Montréal et qui était revenu au pays pour travailler dans une campagne de reforestation. Il nous a parlé des programmes canadiens d'immigration pour les réfugiés. Nous étions dans les derniers spasmes d'une guerre qui s'achevait, et l'idée de tout quitter pour recommencer ailleurs nous a gagnés. Mais le sentiment de m'éloigner peut-être pour toujours de la tombe de ma femme et de mon fils m'angoissait.

Benoît nous a aidés à remplir la paperasse interminable que nous demandait le gouvernement canadien. En mars 1992, nous avons reçu la confirmation que nous pourrions prendre la route de Montréal, tous frais payés. Un avion décollerait de Dakar un mois plus tard, avec moi et ma fille à bord. Le compte à rebours était commencé.

Je me suis mis à tout vendre, à la hâte et au rabais. Un dimanche de la fin mars, quand il ne nous restait presque rien, j'ai décidé d'aller visiter le baobab sacré avec Aïssé. Nous sommes arrivés tôt le matin. Les visiteurs et les curieux n'étaient pas encore là. Je n'avais jamais vu un baobab aussi majestueux. Il éclipsait le ciel, il semblait s'avancer vers nous avec ses énormes racines nues.

On ne parlait pas, Aïssé et moi. On était envahis d'une tristesse sèche, brutale. On comprenait tous les deux, sans dire un mot, qu'on quittait nos morts.

On s'est assis par terre, le dos appuyé contre le tronc. Je me suis mis à penser à l'enfance de Babacar et Aïssé à Diawara, à notre vie de famille. Pour un moment, les souvenirs heureux ont pris le dessus et je me suis assoupi. Quand je me suis réveillé quelques minutes plus tard, j'avais un fruit de baobab dans la main, ce que chez nous on appelle parfois un « pain de singe ».

Le petit baobab que tu as devant toi a poussé à partir d'une semence de ce fruit que j'ai apporté avec moi au Québec, cachée au fond de ma valise. C'était important pour moi : j'avais rêvé une dernière fois de Babacar et Coumba heureux sous ce baobab, et vers la fin de mon rêve, l'arbre avait laissé ce fruit sur ma main.

Le petit baobab que tu as devant toi, c'est le fils du baobab sacré de Fadial. Je l'ai planté ici pour que personne ne le voie. Je l'ai arrosé avec les seules larmes que je verse parfois quand je pense à tout ce qu'on a dû laisser derrière nous.

Je te le montre aujourd'hui pour qu'il puisse t'aider à continuer ton chemin, comme son père m'a aidé il y a 30 ans.

*

Note de l'auteur : Je n'ai jamais rencontré Leopoldo, mais des amis argentins qui l'ont connu m'ont confirmé qu'il vit aujourd'hui en Afrique subsaharienne, où il mène des recherches sur l'adaptation des baobabs aux changements climatiques. En fait, la trame de cette histoire m'a été transmise par ma nouvelle collègue Aïssé, la fille d'Abdourahmane, lors d'une longue marche sur les berges de Verdun, quartier que nous habitons tous les deux.

Les vides, les détails manquants de la trame, se sont remplis seuls au fil des semaines qui ont suivi notre conversation, mon imagination découplée par les mille senteurs qui montaient vers moi des eaux troubles des rapides de Lachine, pendant que j'écrivais ces lignes assis sur un banc de parc, face à la petite île Rock où — j'en suis maintenant convaincu — un baobab a un jour poussé.

***

Acknowledgements

We are truly grateful to all the contributors, to our editor Ángel Mota Berriozábal, to Dara Armsden Ridell (Head of Education and Outreach at the Art Gallery of Alberta), to Dominic Godbout (winner of our cover design contest), to our English copy editor Ellen Kartz, to our French copy editor Jean-Pierre Pelletier, to our proofreader Alicia Chantal (Fresh Look Editing), and designers Leslie Irvine (for our new and bold press logo) and Cecilia Salcedo (our cover and book designer). Thank you for sharing your talents with us!

About the Editor

Né au Mexique, Ángel Mota Berriozábal a un Doctorat en littérature comparée, Université de Montréal. Il a été chroniqueur à la radio et à la télévision hispaniques à Montréal. Angel a co-édité les revues *Enfasis*, *Hélios*, *Vice-Versa* et *Apostles Review* (Montréal). Il est éditeur invité à la maison d'édition Laberinto Press. Commissaire littéraire de la *Fondation LatinArte* et organisateur des tables rondes, des événements littéraires, des conférences et des lectures. Ses poèmes et nouvelles ont été publiés dans des magazines et des livres collectifs au Canada, en Espagne, aux États-Unis, au Mexique, en Italie, en France et au Chili.

Born in Mexico, Laberinto Press guest editor Ángel Mota Berriozábal has a Ph.D. in Comparative Literature from the University of Montreal. He was a columnist on Hispanic radio and television, also in Montreal. Angel has co-edited *Enfasis*, *Hélios*, *Vice-Versa* and *Apostles Review*. He is literary curator of the *LatinArte Foundation*, where he organizes round tables, literary events, conferences, and readings. His poems and short stories have been published in magazines and collections in Canada, Spain, the United States, Mexico, Italy, France, and Chile.

Designer's Note

As a frequent collaborator of Laberinto Press, I was excited to get to work when Luciana called me to work on this iteration of the Beyond series: *Beyond the Park*. Community partners at the Art Gallery of Alberta invited children aged four to seven years old to submit a piece of art on the subject of "The Park." The winning entry, a sparkling collage of shapes in green and yellow suns and trees by Dominic Godbout landed on my desk as the starting point for the design of *Beyond the Park*. His work brings a childlike sense of wonder and freedom to the anthology. I was inspired by his use of colour and hand cut shapes that form a nature scene. I couldn't help but think about the sheets of paper he would have used to cut out forms that went on to become his piece. To the left you can start to see that idea coming to life; we start to see the negative space these shapes left behind. What new worlds can be layered, created, discovered? The design behind *Beyond the Park* supports the worlds talented authors have created, all thanks to Dominic and his creative explorations.

———

Cecilia Salcedo
Graphic Designer

Artwork by Dominic Godbout